# You Will Be My Witnesses

Music for Christian Initiation
by
The Collegeville Composers Group

LITURGICAL PRESS
Collegeville, Minnesota

www.litpress.org

## ADDITIONAL RESOURCES

A separate edition for cantors and choirs is available from Liturgical Press, item number 978-0-8146-3344-1. A CD recording is also available, item number 978-0-8146-7969-2.

## ACKNOWLEDGEMENTS

Music from *You Will Be My Witnesses: Music for Christian Initiation* © 2010, The Collegeville Composers Group (Carol Browning, Catherine Christmas, Cyprian Consiglio, O.S.B. Cam., Paul F. Ford, Ph.D., Paul Inwood). Published and administered by Liturgical Press, Collegeville, Minnesota 56321. All rights reserved.

Cover design by Ann Blattner. Cover image: istockphoto.com.



ISBN 978-0-8146-3343-4

# Contents

# Come, Children, Listen to Me

Rite of Acceptance into the Order of Catechumens:
Entry into the Church

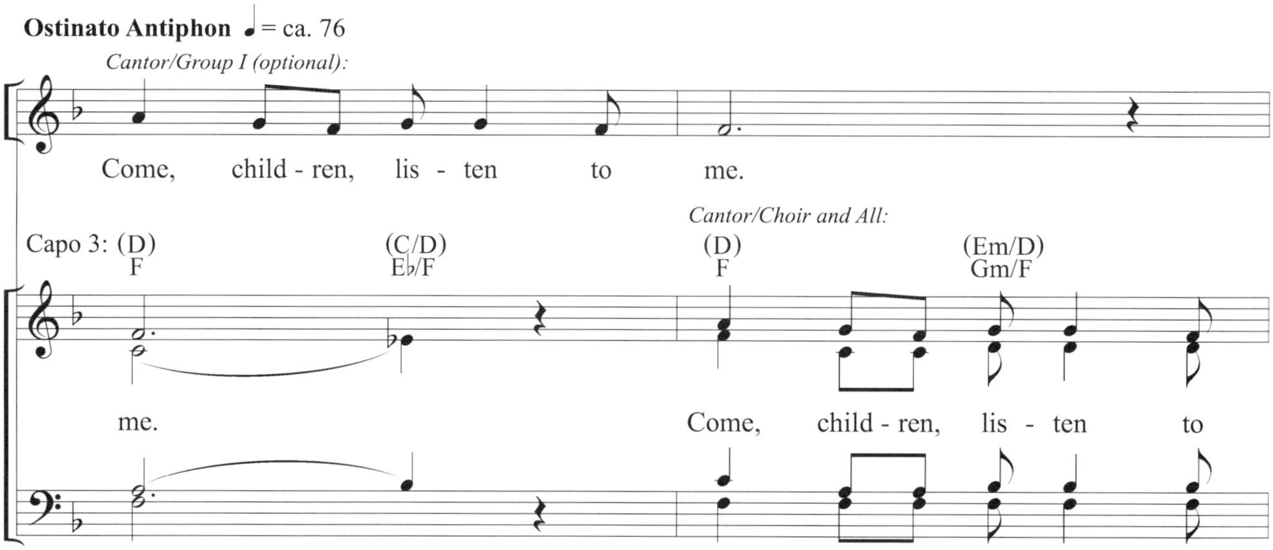


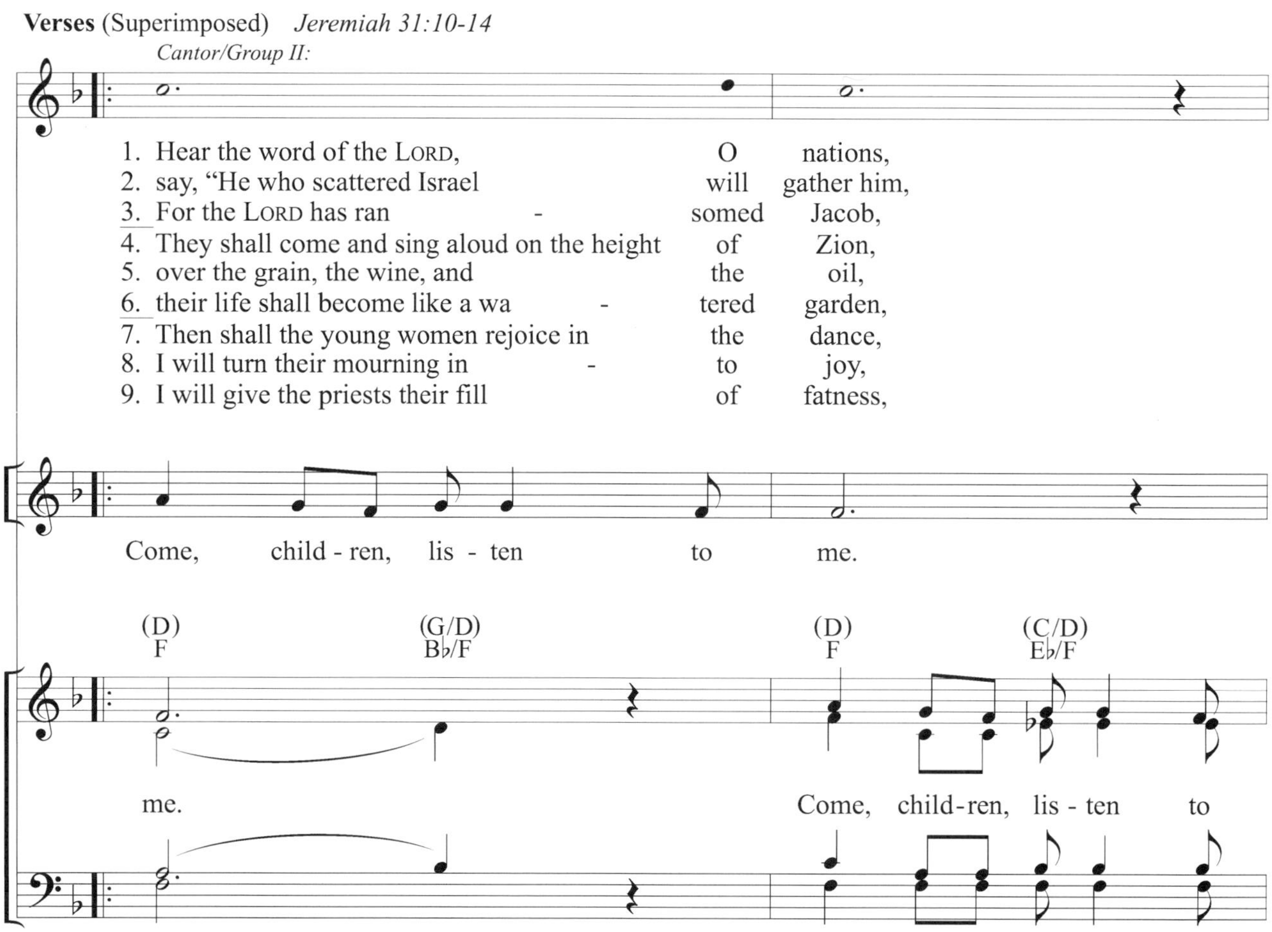

**Performance Notes**

*Each phrase of the ostinato antiphon is first sung by a cantor or small group of unison voices, then repeated in unison (or in harmony) by all. (If only one cantor or unison group is available, the overlap-echo of the antiphon is optional.) The assembly continues to sing the ostinato refrain once it has been intoned.*

*The superimposed verses are sung by a solo cantor or small group of unison voices. The ostinato antiphon should be well established before beginning the verses.*

*This piece may be sung a half-step lower in E (guitars = Capo 2).*

# Lord, We Praise You

Rite of Acceptance into the Order of Catechumens:
Affirmation by the Sponsors and the Assembly

**Invocations**

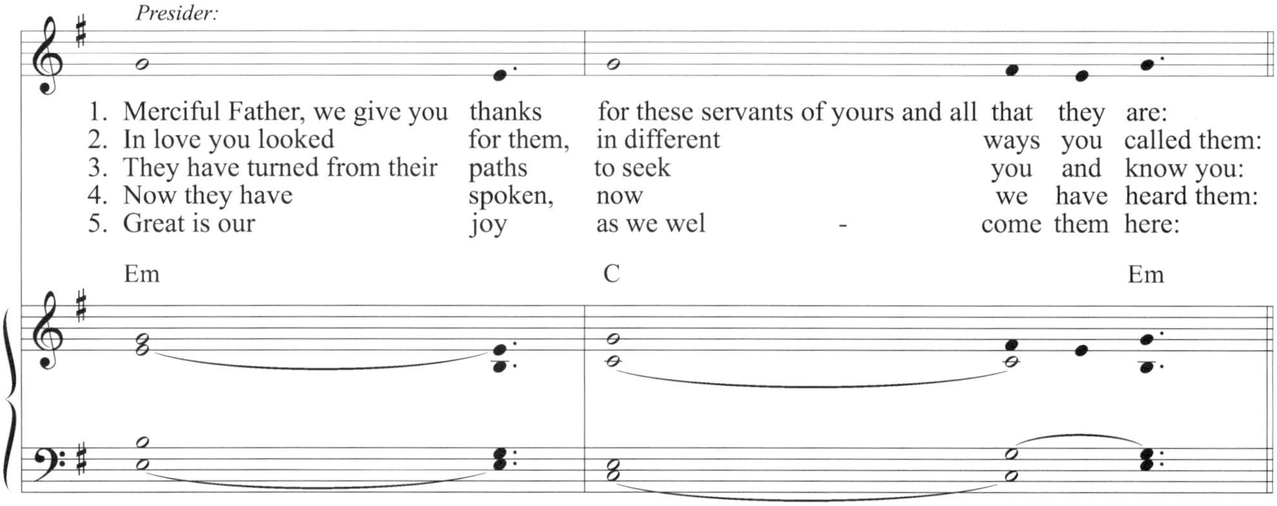


**Response** ♩ = ca. 76

# We Adore You, O Christ, and We Praise You

Rite of Acceptance into the Order of Catechumens:
Signing of the Senses

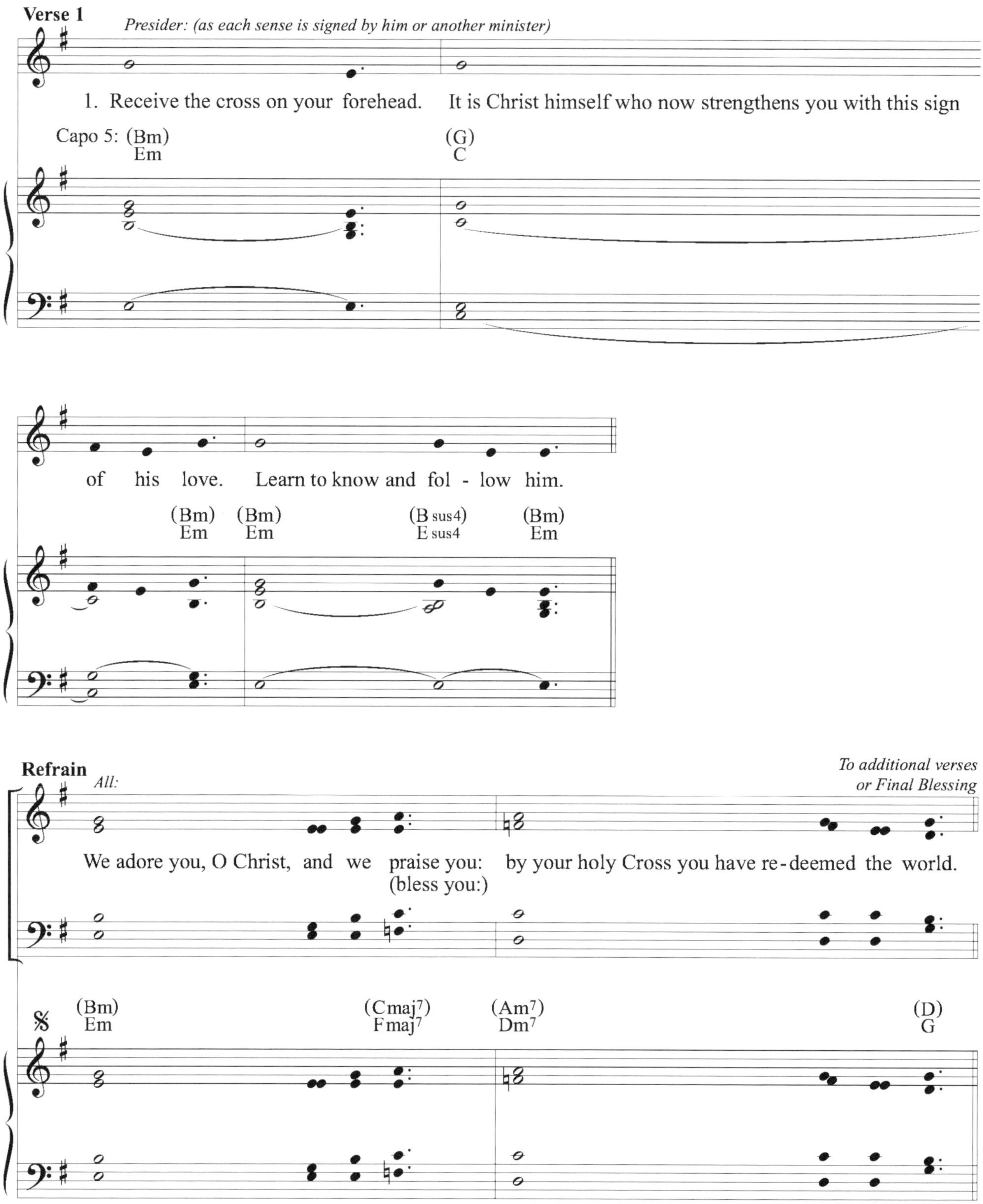

**Verses 2–8**

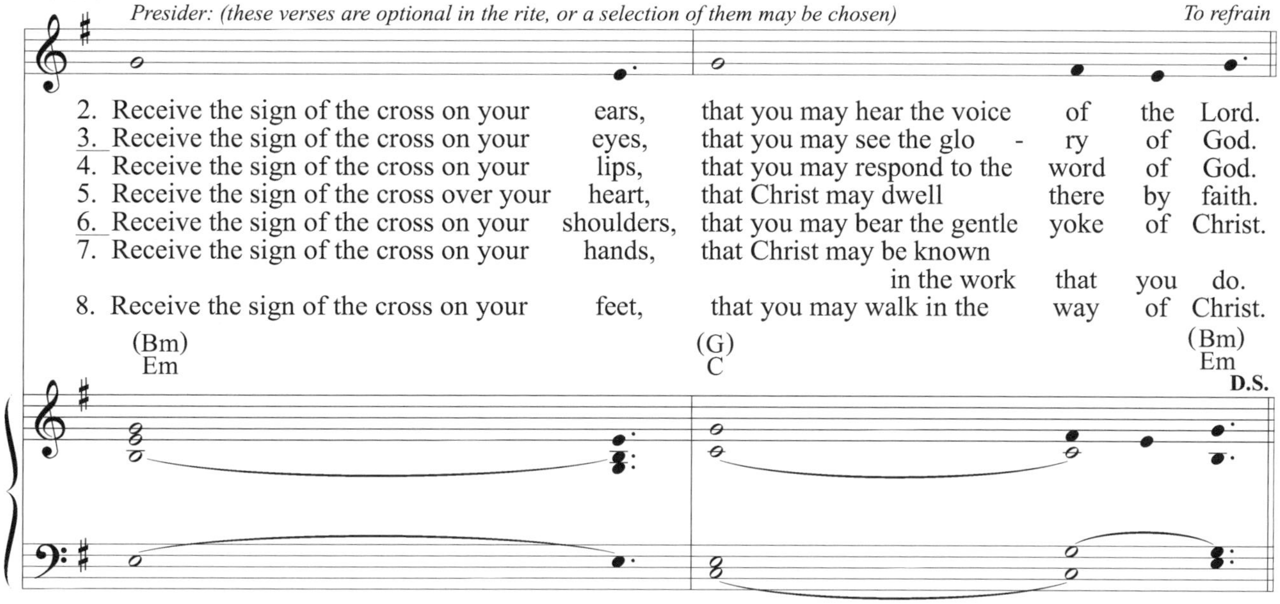


**Final Blessing**

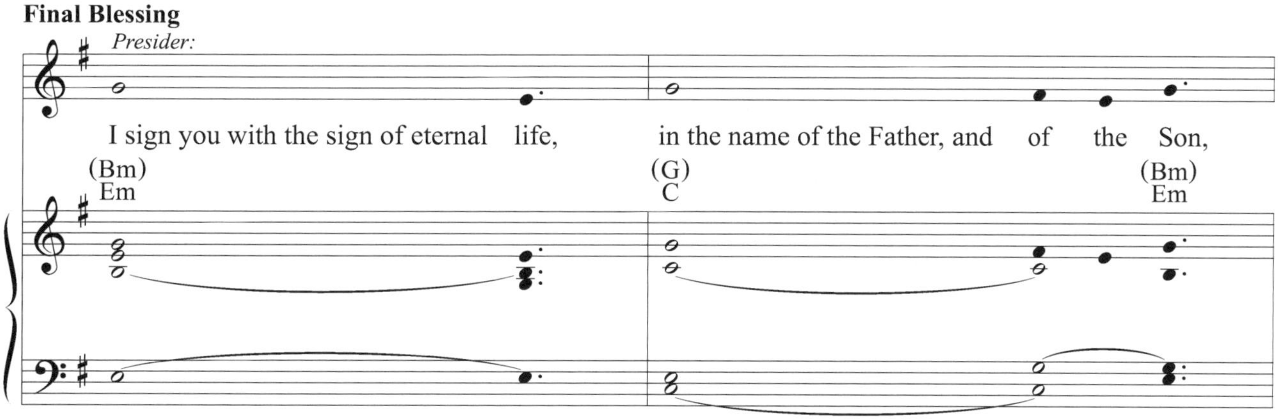


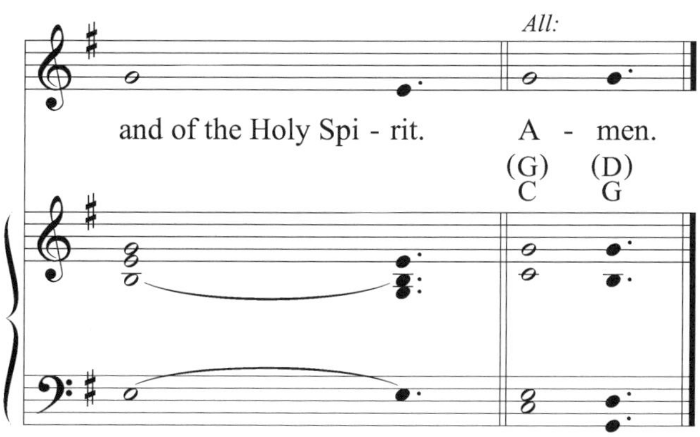


**Performance Notes**

*After the senses have been signed, the presider alone may make the sign of the cross over all the candidates at once, without touching them, and singing the blessing. If there are more than two or three candidates and the decision is taken to bless them individually instead of collectively, it may be preferable for the blessing to be spoken rather than sung.*
*The refrain may also be used during the Stations of the Cross (using the alternate words in parentheses).*

# Go in Peace

Rite of Christian Initiation of Adults:
Dismissal of the Catechumens

**Invocations**

*Presider:*

| | | | | |
|---|---|---|---|---|
| 1. | Go now in peace, beloved | ca - | te - | chumens. |
| *or* | Go now in peace, be - | lov - | ed | friends. |
| 2. | May the Lord's peace remain | with | you | always. |
| 3. | Feed on God's word, and grow | in | God's | strength. |
| 4. | One day, we pray, you will share | the | Lord's | table. |
| | *Additional invocations during Lent and other times* | | | |
| 5. | May God create a pure heart in you and | give | you | help. |
| 6. | May you be nourished not on bread alone but on every | word | from | God. |
| 7. | May you be the beloved of the Lord, and rejoice | in | his | favor. |
| 8. | May the Lord, the savior of the world, give you the | liv - | ing | water. |
| 9. | Follow the light of the world and have the | light | of | life. |
| 10. | Believe in Jesus, the resurrection | and | the | life. |
| 11. | Believe in God's only Son and have e - | ter - | nal | life. |
| 12. | May you follow the Lord and re - | joice | in | serving him. |
| 13. | Repent, for the kingdom of heaven is | close | at | hand. |
| 14. | Acknowledge your sins, and find joy | in | God's | mercy. |
| 15. | Seek good and not evil, and the God of hosts | will | be | with you. |
| 16. | Listen always to the voice | of | the | Lord. |
| 17. | Be open to a heart and a spirit | that | are | new. |
| 18. | Count on God's mercy and fullness | of | re - | demption. |
| 19. | Be noble and generous, and yield a harvest through your | per - | se - | verance. |
| | *Additional invocations for general use* | | | |
| 20. | Keep the word of God, that the Father may love | you | and | dwell with you. |
| 21. | May God make you holy | in | the | truth. |
| 22. | May your heart(s) be open to hear the words | of | God's | Son. |
| 23. | May the Father of our Lord Jesus Christ enlighten the eyes | of | your | mind. |
| 24. | Stay awake | and | stand | ready! |
| 25. | Keep faithful, that you may receive the | crown | of | life. |

**Response** ♩ = ca. 58, *rall.* to ♩ = ca. 50 in second half

**Performance Notes**

*Verses 1–4 are for general use, derived from the rite itself. Others may be selected from those given above, derived from the Sunday Gospel Acclamations for Lent and Ordinary Time, or you can write your own. Use as many verses as necessary to cover the departure of the catechumens - four verses would be a good minimum.*

*This setting can also be used as a recessional song at the end of Mass, following the dismissal by the deacon/priest, as well as at other blessing occasions.*

# Glory to You, Lord Jesus Christ

Lenten Gospel Acclamation

**Performance Notes**

*For a short acclamation, sing once through. For a more extended gospel procession, use 'invocations' 2 and 3 of the refrain in addition.*

*Percussion will be of great help in establishing the rhythm of this 7/8 piece.*

# Lord, Listen to Our Prayer

Intercessions Litany for the First Scrutiny

**Invocations** (two options)

*Minister/Cantor:*

1A. That they may ponder the word of God in their hearts
2A. That they may learn to know Christ,
3A. *[begins in measure 2]*
4A. That they may sincerely reject everything in their lives
5A. That the Holy Spirit, who searches e - v'ry heart,
6A. That the same Holy Spirit may teach them to know the things of God,
7A. That their families also may put their hope in Christ
8A. That we ourselves in preparation for the Easter feast may seek a change of heart,
9A. That throughout the whole world whatever is weak may be strengthened, whatever is bro - ken re - stored,

1B. That, like the woman of Samaria, our elect may review their lives be - fore Christ
2B. That they may be freed from the spirit of mis - trust
3B. That, while awaiting the gift of God,
4B. That, by accepting the Son of God as their teacher,
5B. That they may share with their friends and neighbors
6B. That those whose lives are empty for want of the word of God
7B. That all of us may learn from Christ

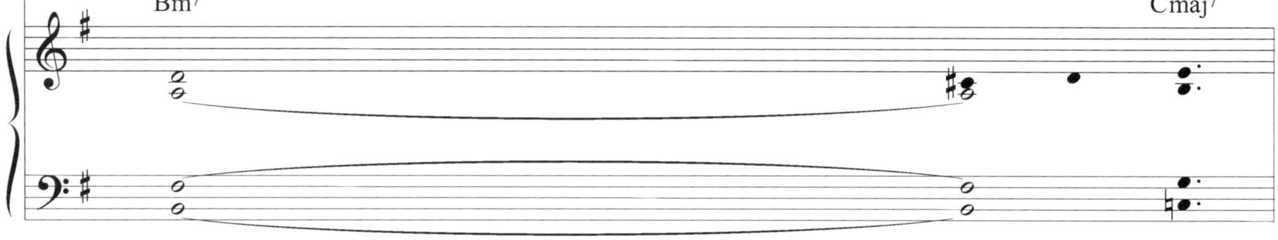


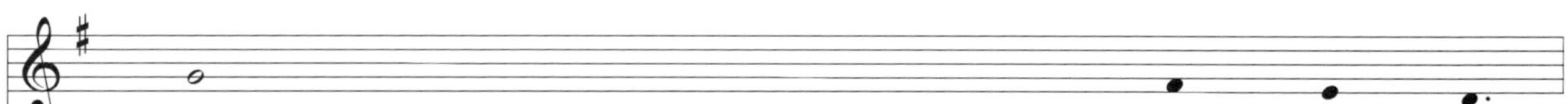

1A. and savor its meaning more fully day by day,
2A. who came to save what was lost,
3A. That they may humbly confess themselves to be sinners,
4A. that is displeasing and contra - ry to Christ,
5A. may help them to overcome their weakness through his power,
6A. and how to please him,
7A. and find peace and holi - ness in him,
8A. give ourselves to prayer, and persevere in our good works,
9A. whatever is lost found, and what is found re - deemed,

1B. and acknow - ledge their sins,
2B. that deters people from fol - low - ing Christ,
3B. they may long with all their hearts for the living water that brings e - ter - nal life,
4B. they may become true worshipers of the Father in spirit and in truth,
5B. the wonder of their own meet - ing with Christ,
6B. may come to the Gos - pel of Christ,
7B. to do the Father's will in love,

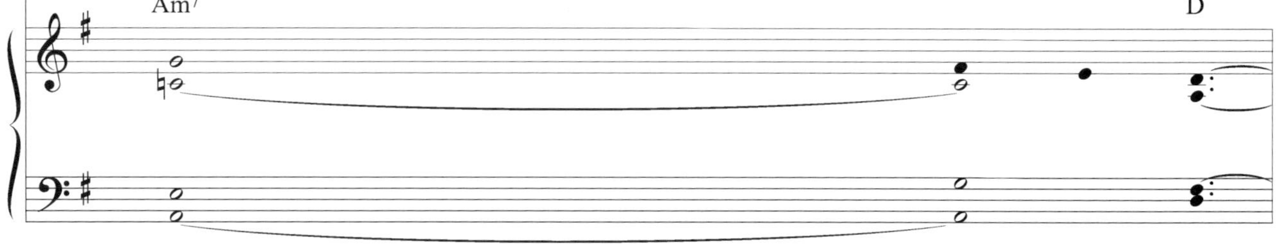

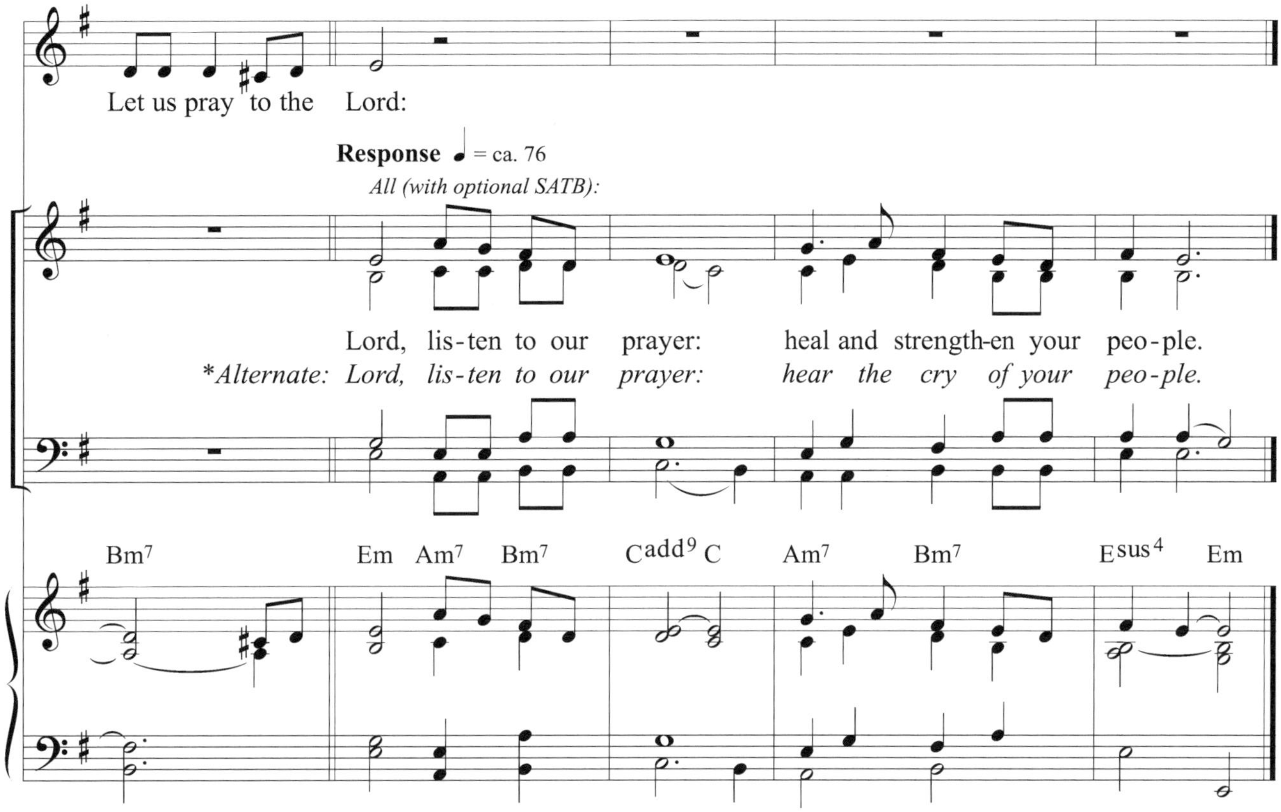


**Performance Notes**

*Intercessions may also be adapted to include specific intentions of each community - for example, intentions naming those who have died.*

*This setting may also be found suitable, using different invocations, for use in services of healing and reconciliation.*

**Alternate setting: by changing the response text to* Lord, listen to our prayer: hear the cry of your people *the setting may also be found useful for general intercessions during other liturgical seasons/times.*

# Lord, Listen to Our Prayer

Intercessions Litany for the Second Scrutiny

**Invocations** (two options)

*Minister/Cantor:*

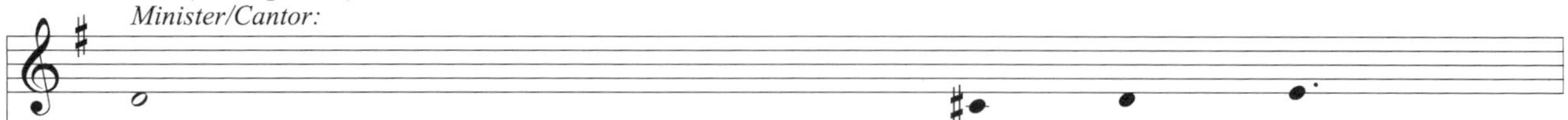

1A. That, trusting in the truth of Christ,
2A. That, preferring the folly of the cross to the wisdom of the world,
3A. That, freed by the power of the Spirit,
4A. That, transformed in the Spirit,
5A. That all who suffer persecution for Christ's name
6A. That those families and nations prevented from embracing the faith
7A. That we who are faced with the values of the world
8A. That the whole world, which the Father so loves,

1B. That God may dispel darkness
2B. That he may gently lead them to Christ,
3B. That our elect may open their hearts to God
4B. That he may heal them and preserve them
5B. That, saved by him who takes the sin of the world,
6B. That, enlightened by the Holy Spirit,
7B. That all of us, by the example of our lives,
8B. That every inhabitant of the earth

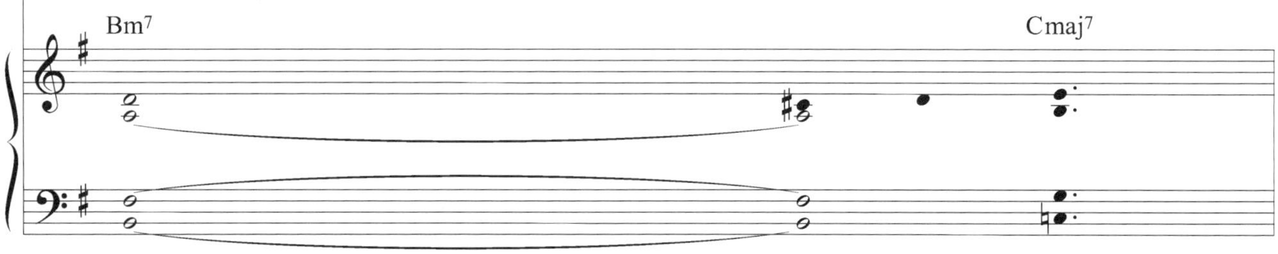


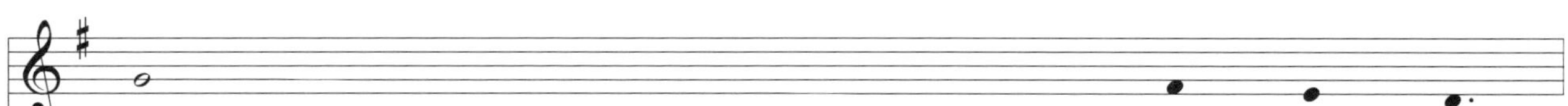

1A. they may find freedom of mind and heart and preserve it always,
2A. they may glory in God alone,
3A. they may put all fear behind them and press forward with confidence,
4A. they may seek those things that are holy and just,
5A. may find their strength in him,
6A. may be granted freedom to believe the Gospel,
7A. may remain faithful to the spirit of the Gospel,
8A. may attain in the Church complete spiritual freedom,

1B. and be the light that shines in the hearts of our elect,
2B. the light of the world,
3B. and acknowledge him as the source of light and the witness of truth,
4B. from the unbelief of this world,
5B. they may be freed from the contagion and forces of sin,
6B. they may never fail to profess the Good News of salvation and share it with others,
7B. may become in Christ the light of the world,
8B. may acknowledge the true God, the Creator of all things,
who bestows on us the gift of Spirit and life,

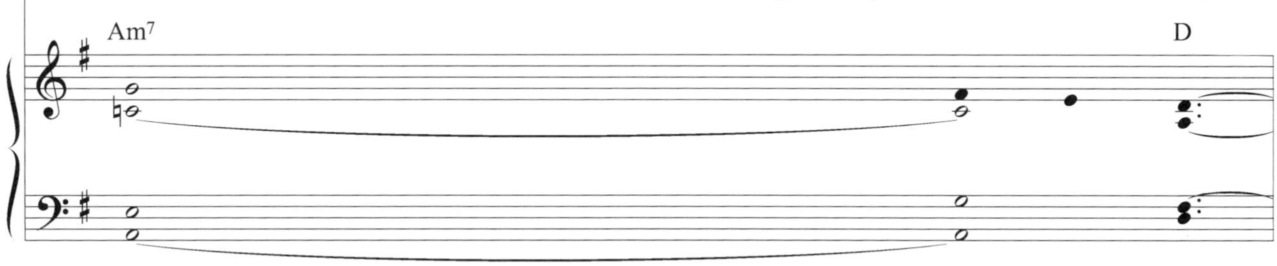

**Performance Notes**

*Intercessions may also be adapted to include specific intentions of each community - for example, intentions naming those who have died.*

*This setting may also be found suitable, using different invocations, for use in services of healing and reconciliation.*

**Alternate setting: by changing the response text to* Lord, listen to our prayer: hear the cry of your people *the setting may also be found useful for general intercessions during other liturgical seasons/times.*

# Lord, Listen to Our Prayer

Intercessions Litany for the Third Scrutiny

**Invocations** (two options)

*Minister/Cantor:*

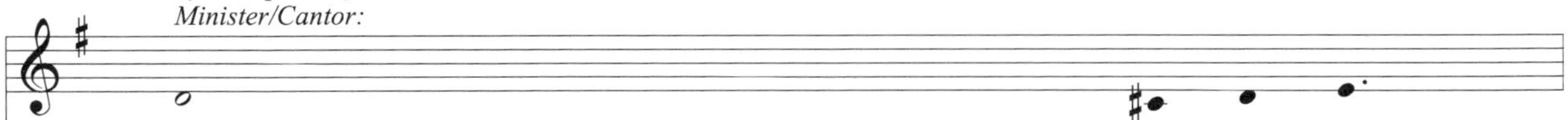

1A. That faith may strengthen them
2A. That they may always thank God,
3A. That the example and prayers of catechumens who have shed their blood for Christ
4A. That they may all have a horror of sin,
5A. That those who are saddened by the death of family or friends
6A. That we too at Easter may again be confirmed
7A. That the whole world, which God has created in love,

1B. That these elect may be given the faith
2B. That they may be freed from sin
3B. That, liberated by repentance from the shackles of sin,
4B. That they may be filled with the hope of the life-giving Spirit
5B. That the eucharistic food, which they are soon to receive,
6B. That all of us may walk in newness of life
7B. That all the world may find Christ

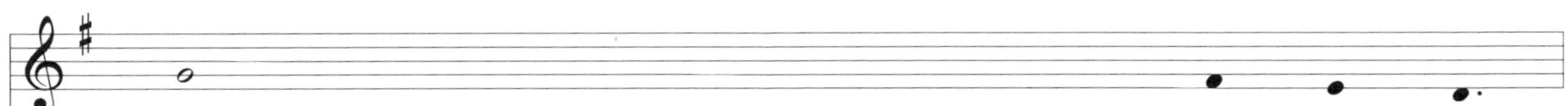

1A. against worldly deceits of ev'ry kind,
2A. who has chosen to rescue them from their ignorance of eternal life and to set them on their way to salvation,
3A. may encourage these elect in their hope of eternal life,
4A. which distorts life,
5A. may find comfort in Christ,
6A. in our hope of rising to life with Christ,
7A. may flower in faith and charity and so receive new life,

1B. to acknowledge Christ as the resurrection and the life,
2B. and grow in the holiness that leads to eternal life,
3B. they may become like Christ in baptism, dead to sin and alive for ever in God's sight,
4B. and prepare themselves thoroughly for their birth to new life,
5B. may make them one with Christ, the source of life and of resurrection,
6B. and show to the world the power of the risen Christ,
7B. and acknowledge in him the promises of eternal life,

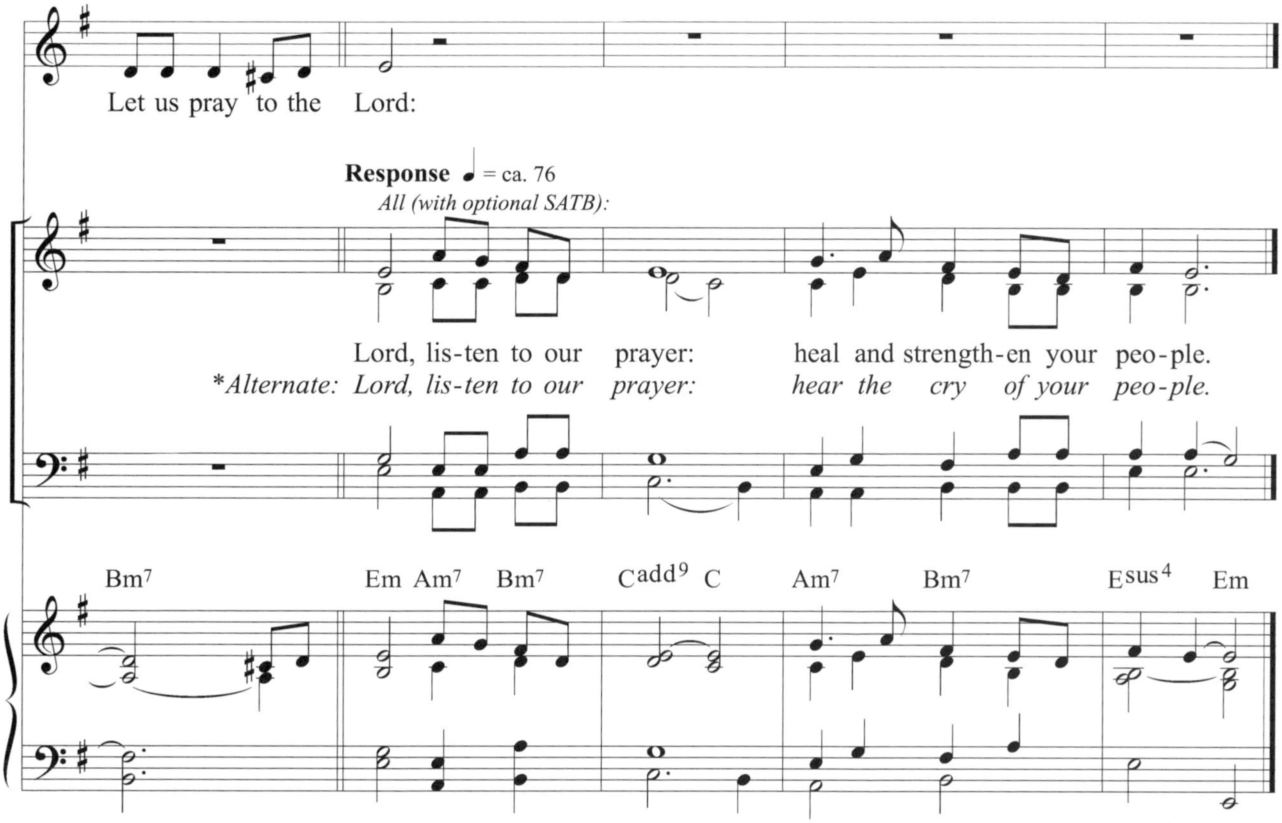


**Performance Notes**

*Intercessions may also be adapted to include specific intentions of each community - for example, intentions naming those who have died.*

*This setting may also be found suitable, using different invocations, for use in services of healing and reconciliation.*

**Alternate setting: by changing the response text to* Lord, listen to our prayer: hear the cry of your people *the setting may also be found useful for general intercessions during other liturgical seasons/times.*

# Apostles' Creed

Latin

**Setting I** (melody in the Tenor line)

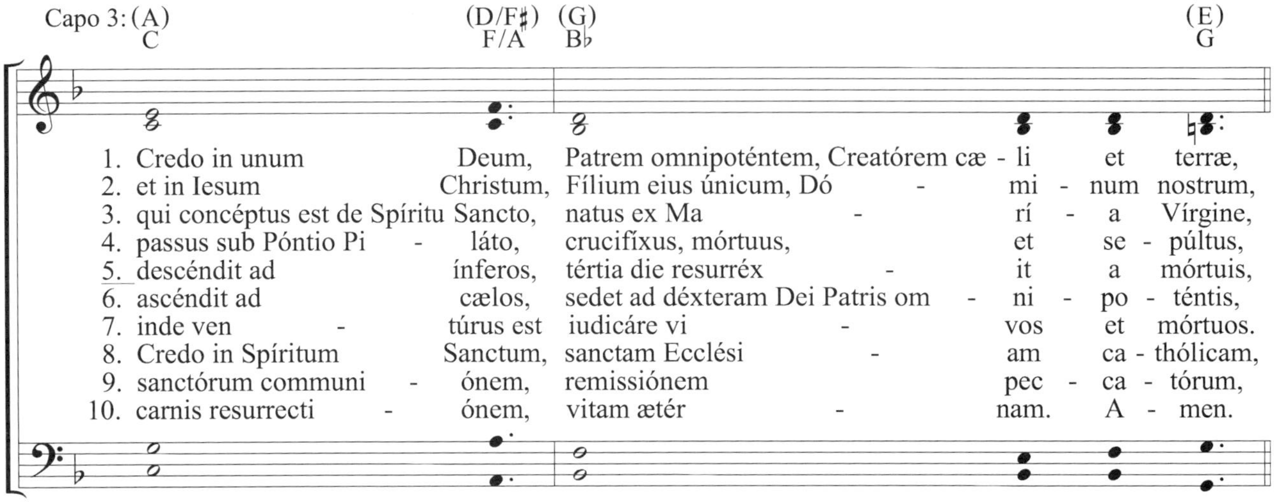


**Setting II** (melody in the Soprano line)

**Performance Notes**

*The chant can be sung as above, with the tenor taking the melody in Setting I, or the soprano in Setting II (SATB). The bass descant remains constant whichever version is used.*

*The odd-numbered verses could be sung by a solo cantor and the even-numbered verses by choir and all; or everyone can sing all the verses throughout.*

*Discreet organ accompaniment may be used to sustain the voices. If guitar is used, only one strum per chord symbol should be played.*

# Apostles' Creed

English

**Setting I** (melody in the Tenor line)

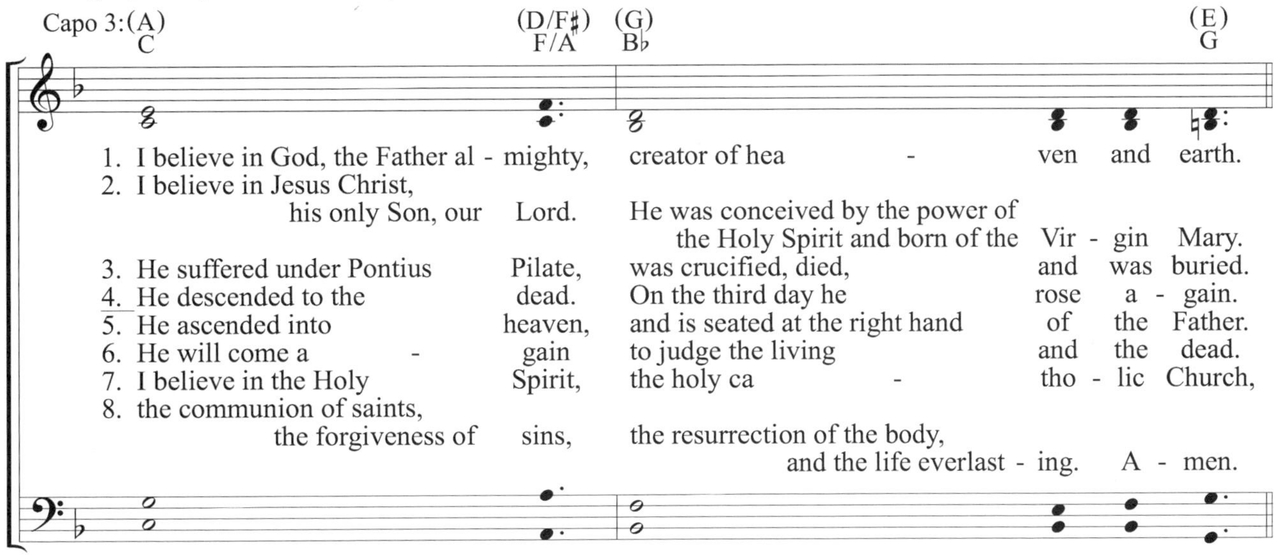


**Setting II** (melody in the Soprano line)

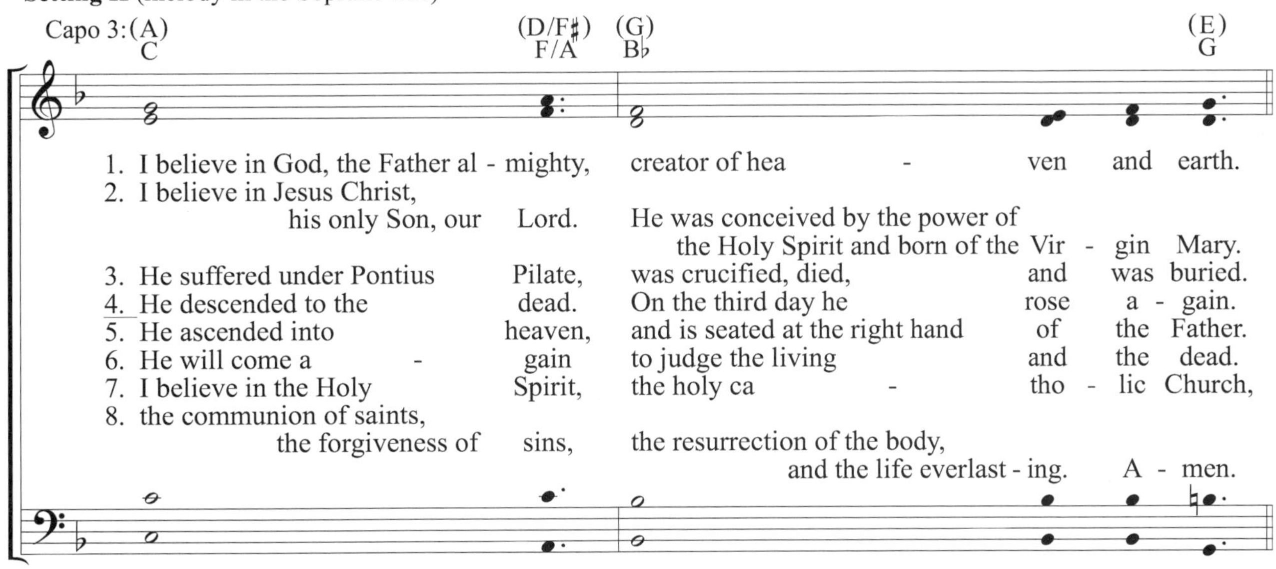


**Performance Notes**

*The chant can be sung as above, with the tenor taking the melody in Setting I, or the soprano in Setting II (SATB). The bass descant remains constant whichever version is used.*

*The odd-numbered verses could be sung by a solo cantor and the even-numbered verses by choir and all; or everyone can sing all the verses throughout.*

*Discreet organ accompaniment may be used to sustain the voices. If guitar is used, only one strum per chord symbol should be played.*

*Another setting of the* Apostles' Creed, *using the new translation from the Order of Mass, is available in the separate collection of music for the Mass written by The Collegeville Composers Group.*

# Apostles' Creed

Spanish

**Setting I** (melody in the Tenor line)

**Setting II** (melody in the Soprano line)

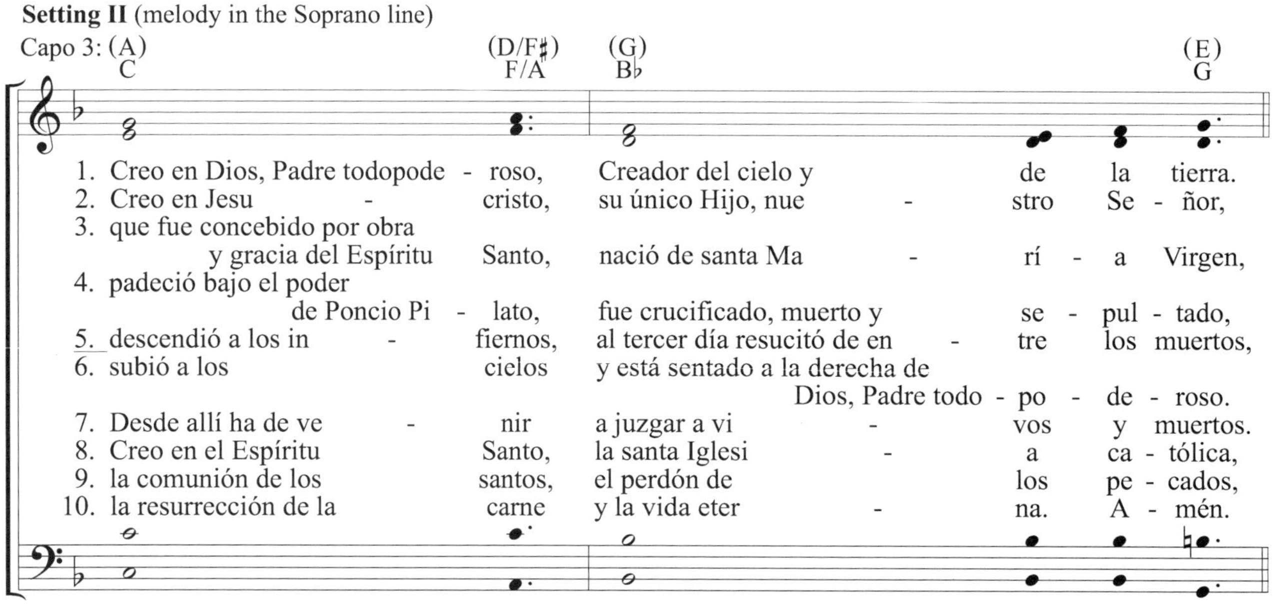


**Performance Notes**

*The chant can be sung as above, with the tenor taking the melody in Setting I, or the soprano in Setting II (SATB). The bass descant remains constant whichever version is used.*

*The odd-numbered verses could be sung by a solo cantor and the even-numbered verses by choir and all; or everyone can sing all the verses throughout.*

*Discreet organ accompaniment may be used to sustain the voices. If guitar is used, only one strum per chord symbol should be played.*

# Nicene Creed

## Latin

**Setting I** (melody in the tenor line)

Capo 3: (A) C — (D/F♯) F/A

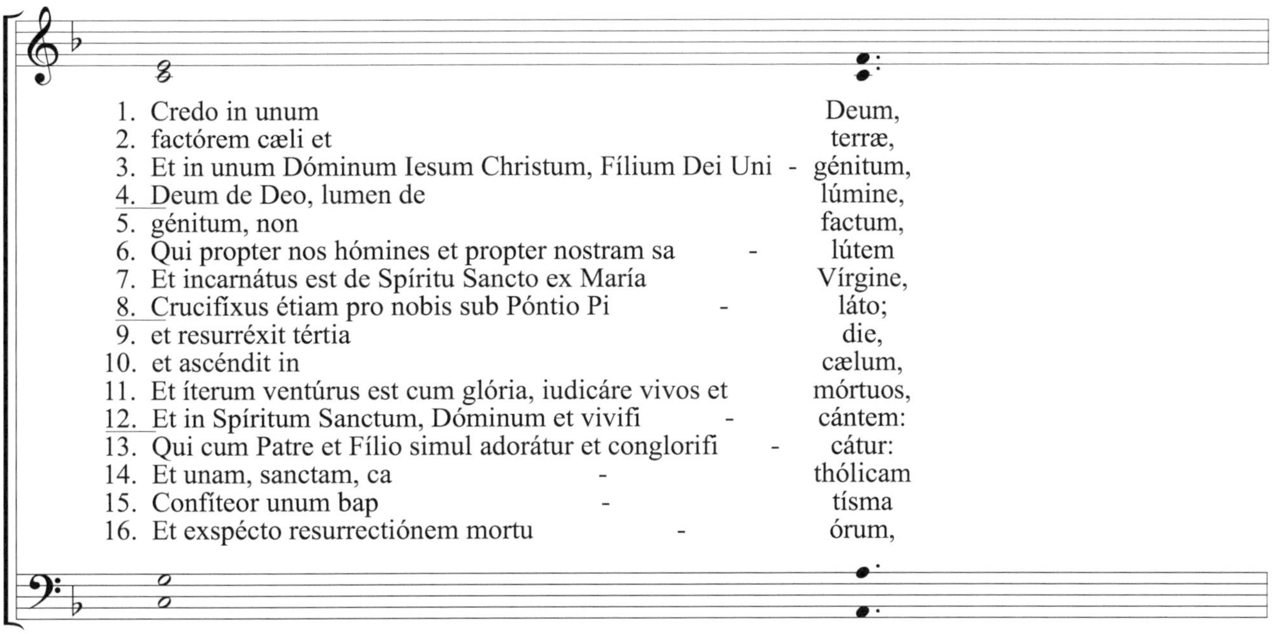

| | | |
|---|---|---|
| 1. | Credo in unum | Deum, |
| 2. | factórem cæli et | terræ, |
| 3. | Et in unum Dóminum Iesum Christum, Fílium Dei Uni - | génitum, |
| 4. | Deum de Deo, lumen de | lúmine, |
| 5. | génitum, non | factum, |
| 6. | Qui propter nos hómines et propter nostram sa - | lútem |
| 7. | Et incarnátus est de Spíritu Sancto ex María | Vírgine, |
| 8. | Crucifíxus étiam pro nobis sub Póntio Pi - | láto; |
| 9. | et resurréxit tértia | die, |
| 10. | et ascéndit in | cælum, |
| 11. | Et íterum ventúrus est cum glória, iudicáre vivos et | mórtuos, |
| 12. | Et in Spíritum Sanctum, Dóminum et vivifi - | cántem: |
| 13. | Qui cum Patre et Fílio simul adorátur et conglorifi - | cátur: |
| 14. | Et unam, sanctam, ca - | thólicam |
| 15. | Confíteor unum bap - | tísma |
| 16. | Et exspécto resurrectiónem mortu - | órum, |

(G) B♭ — (E) G

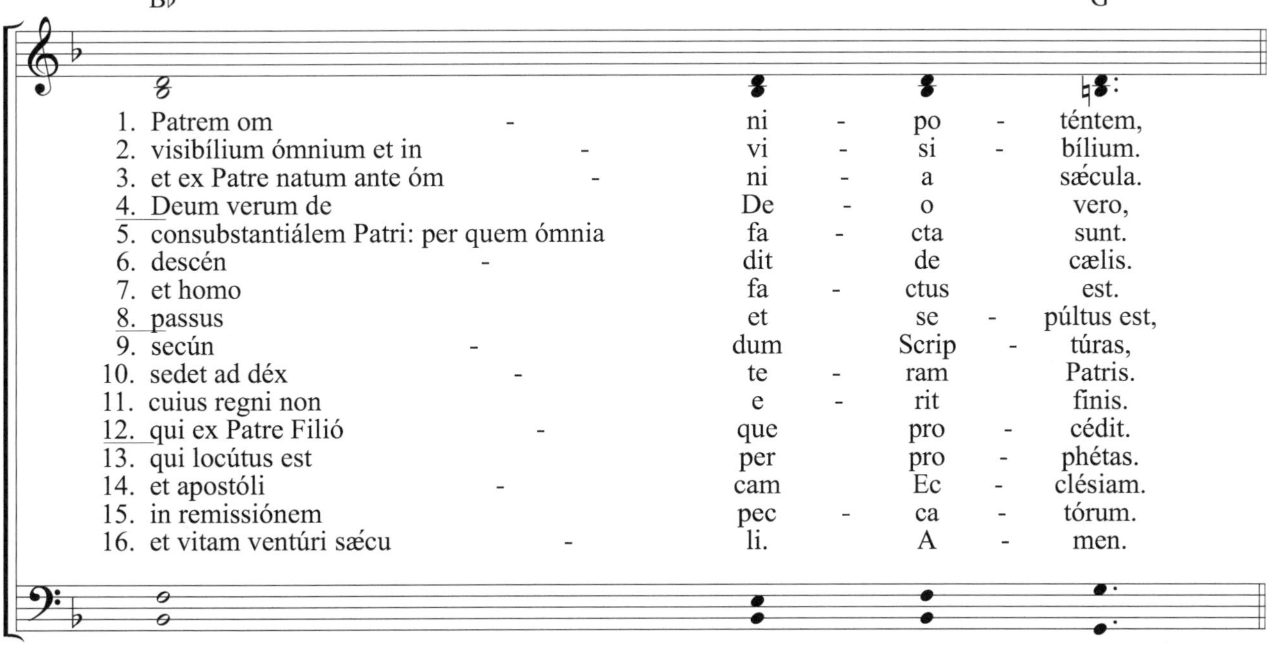

| | | | | |
|---|---|---|---|---|
| 1. | Patrem om - | ni - | po - | téntem, |
| 2. | visibílium ómnium et in - | vi - | si - | bílium. |
| 3. | et ex Patre natum ante óm - | ni - | a | sǽcula. |
| 4. | Deum verum de | De - | o | vero, |
| 5. | consubstantiálem Patri: per quem ómnia | fa - | cta | sunt. |
| 6. | descén - | dit | de | cælis. |
| 7. | et homo | fa - | ctus | est. |
| 8. | passus | et | se - | púltus est, |
| 9. | secún - | dum | Scrip - | túras, |
| 10. | sedet ad déx - | te - | ram | Patris. |
| 11. | cuius regni non | e - | rit | finis. |
| 12. | qui ex Patre Filió - | que | pro - | cédit. |
| 13. | qui locútus est | per | pro - | phétas. |
| 14. | et apostóli - | cam | Ec - | clésiam. |
| 15. | in remissiónem | pec - | ca - | tórum. |
| 16. | et vitam ventúri sǽcu - | li. | A - | men. |

**Setting II** (melody in the soprano line)

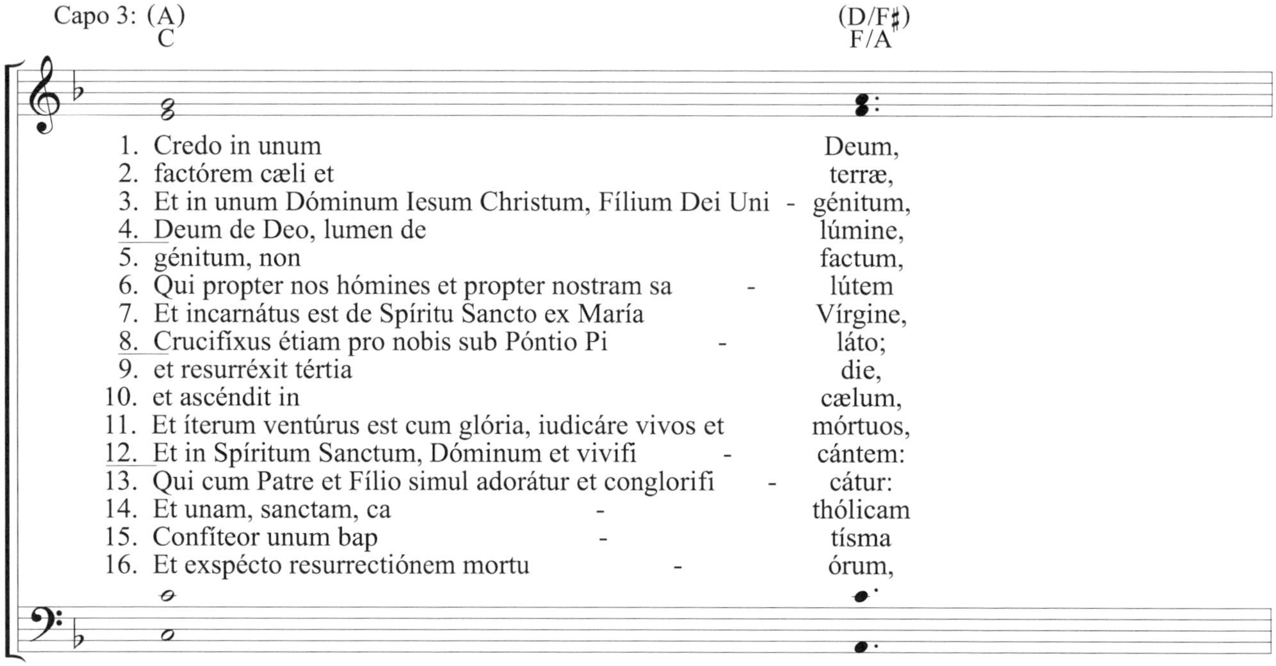


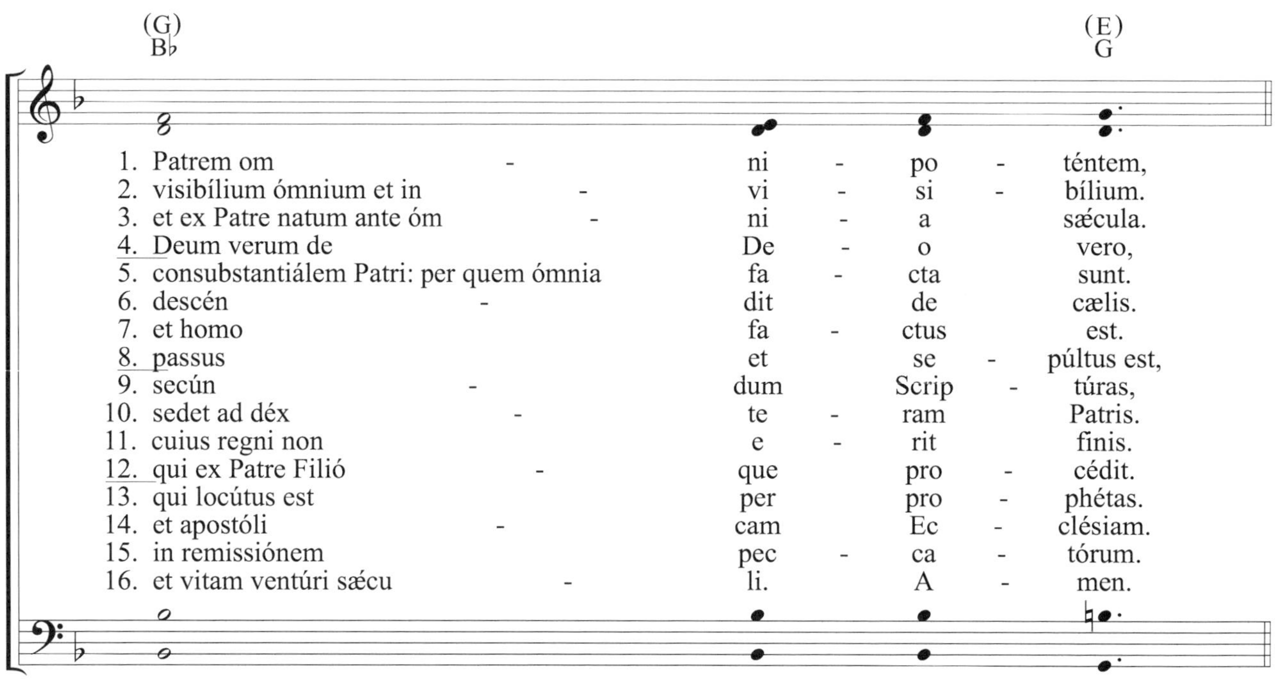


**Performance Notes**

*The chant can be sung with the tenor taking the melody (Setting I), or SATB with the soprano taking the melody (Setting II). The bass descant remains constant whichever version is used.*

*The odd-numbered verses could be sung by a solo cantor and the even-numbered verses by choir and all; or everyone can sing all the verses throughout.*

*Discreet organ accompaniment may be used to sustain the voices. If guitar is used, only one strum per chord symbol should be played.*

# Nicene Creed

English

**Setting I** (melody in the tenor line)

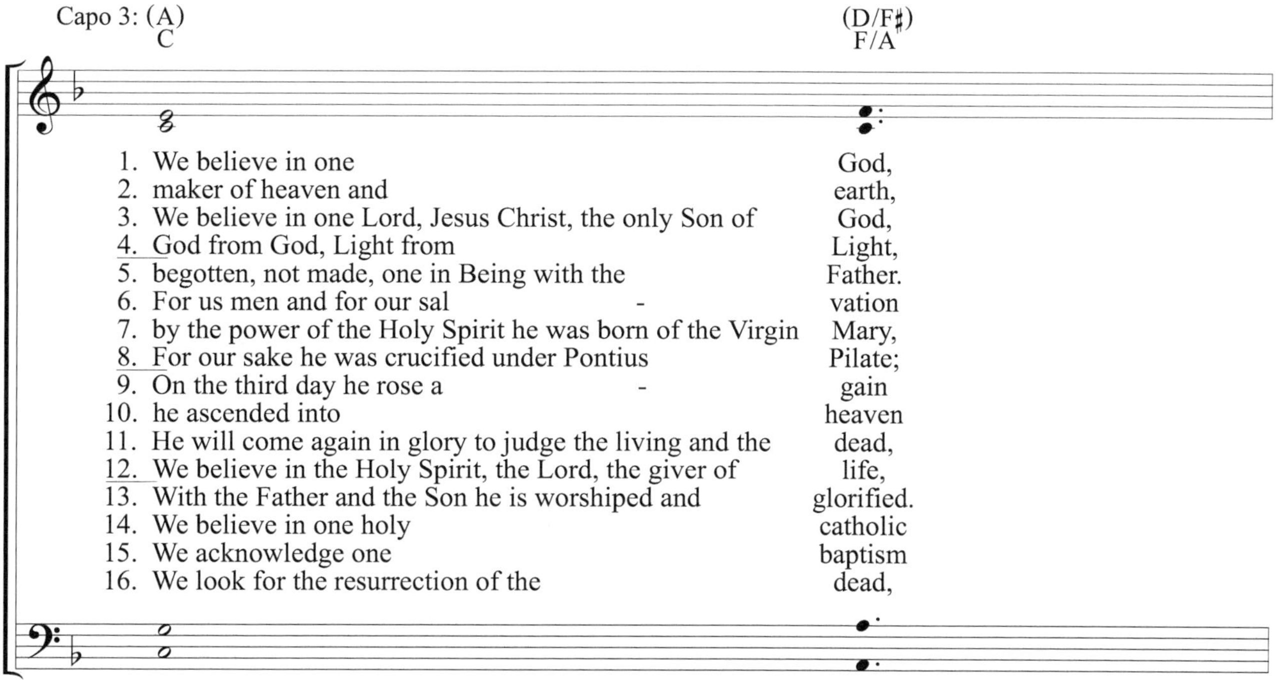


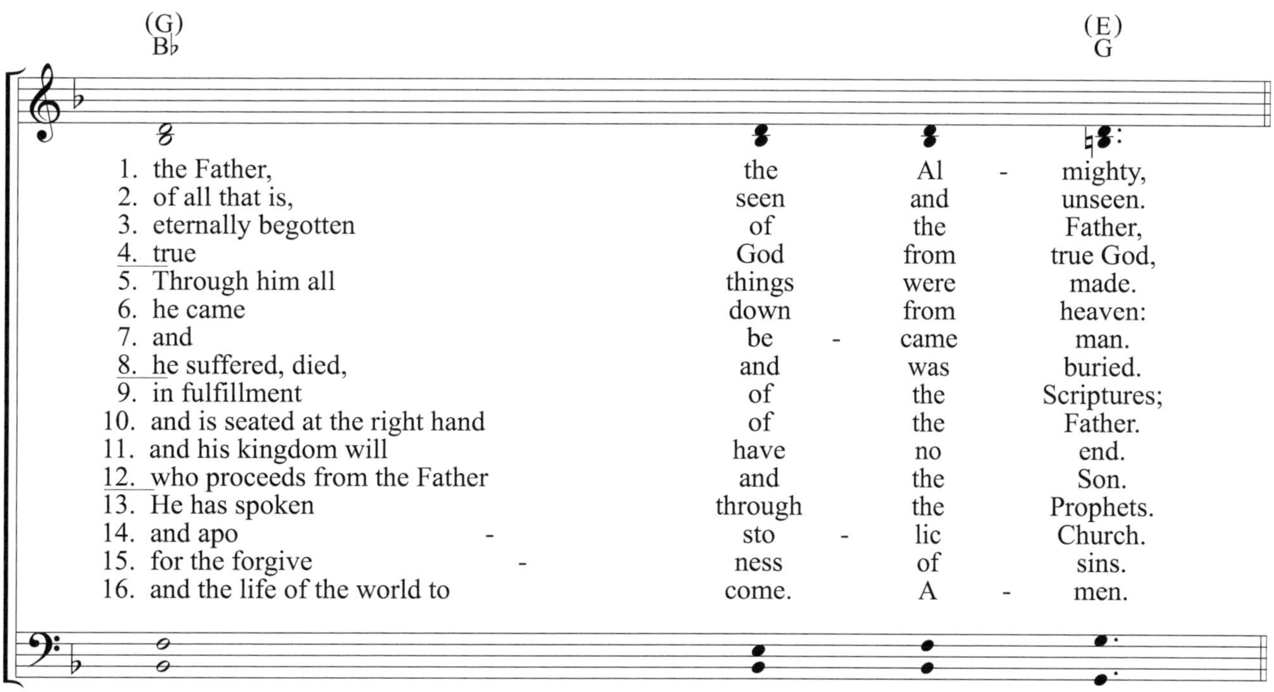

**Setting II** (melody in the soprano line)

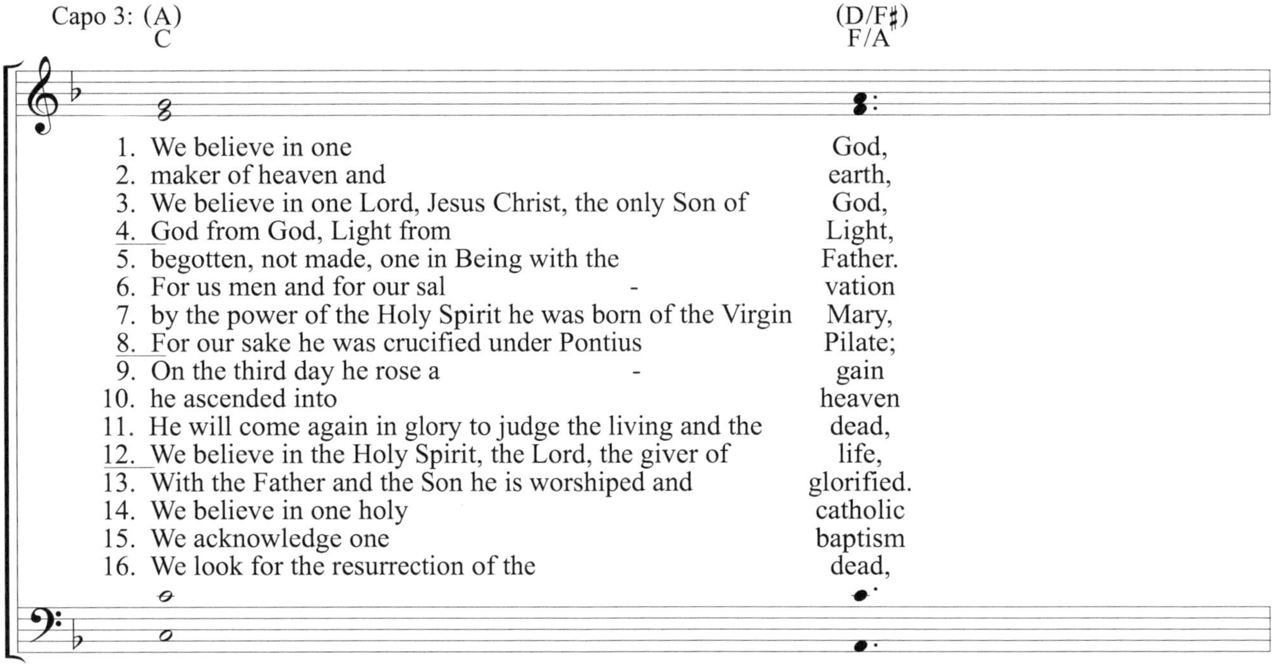


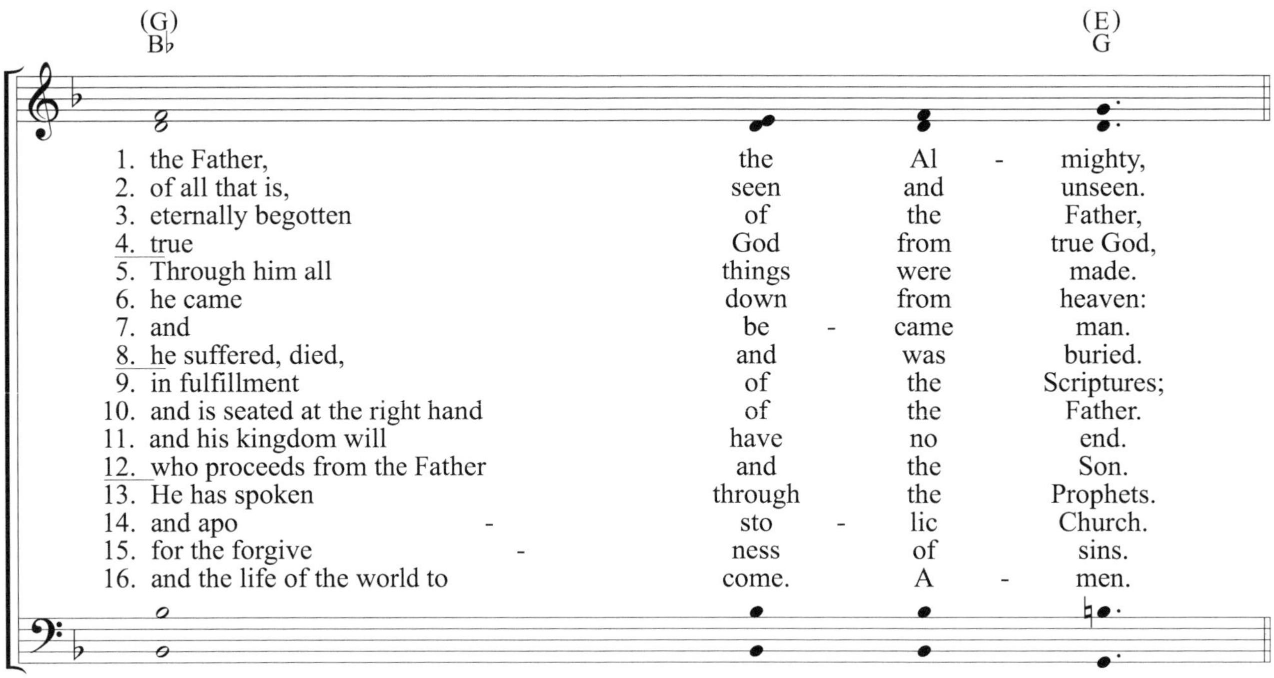


**Performance Notes**

*The chant can be sung with the tenor taking the melody (Setting I), or SATB with the soprano taking the melody (Setting II). The bass descant remains constant whichever version is used.*

*The odd-numbered verses could be sung by a solo cantor and the even-numbered verses by choir and all; or everyone can sing all the verses throughout.*

*Discreet organ accompaniment may be used to sustain the voices. If guitar is used, only one strum per chord symbol should be played.*

*Another setting of the* Nicene Creed, *using the new translation from the Order of Mass, is available in the separate collection of music for the Mass written by The Collegeville Composers Group.*

# Nicene Creed

## Spanish

**Setting I** (melody in the tenor line)

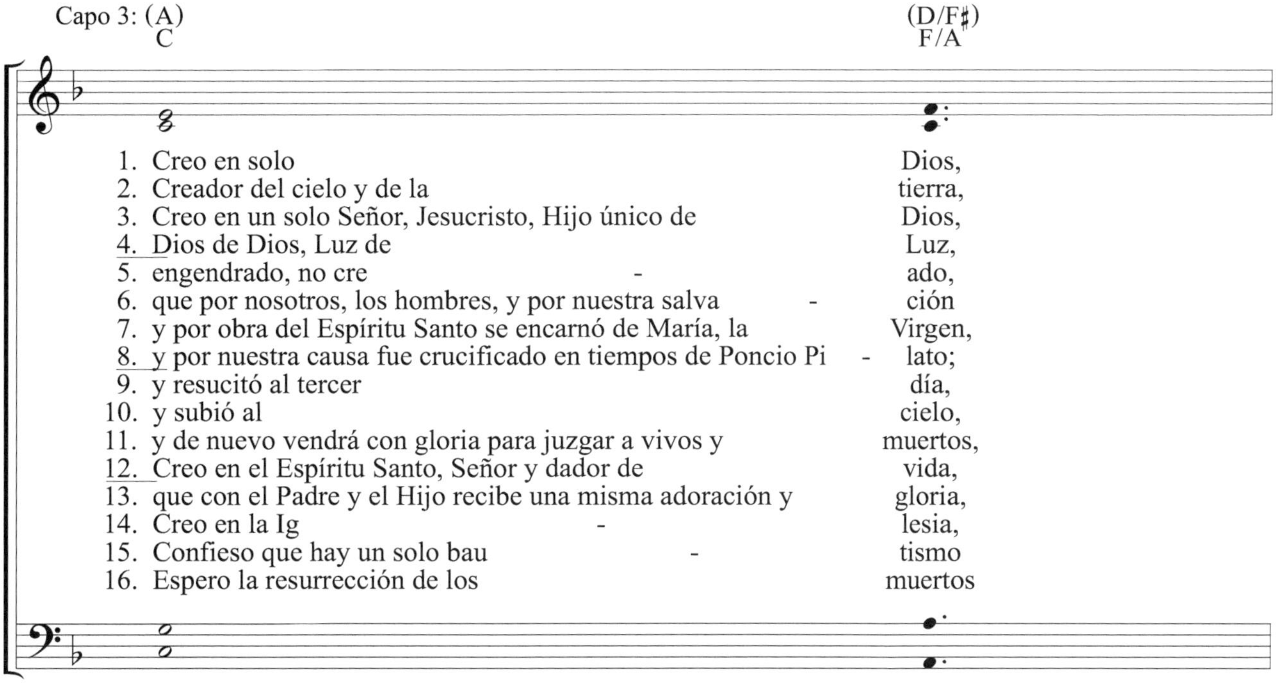


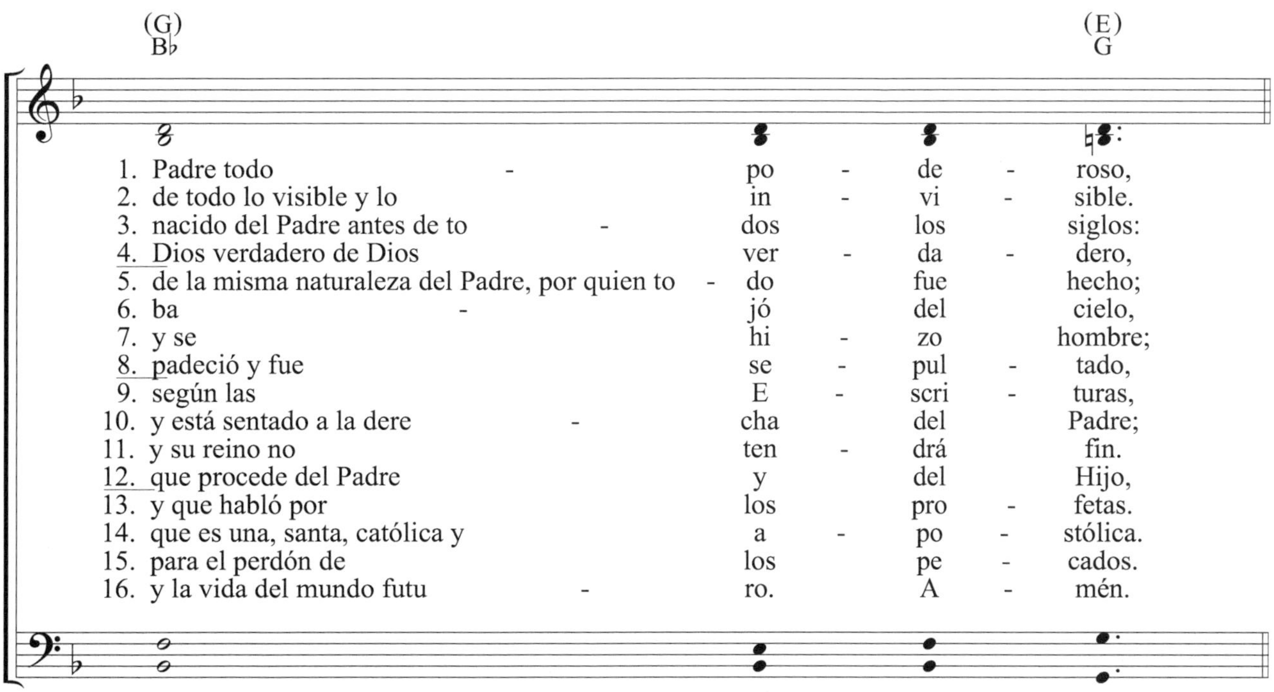

**Setting II** (melody in the soprano line)

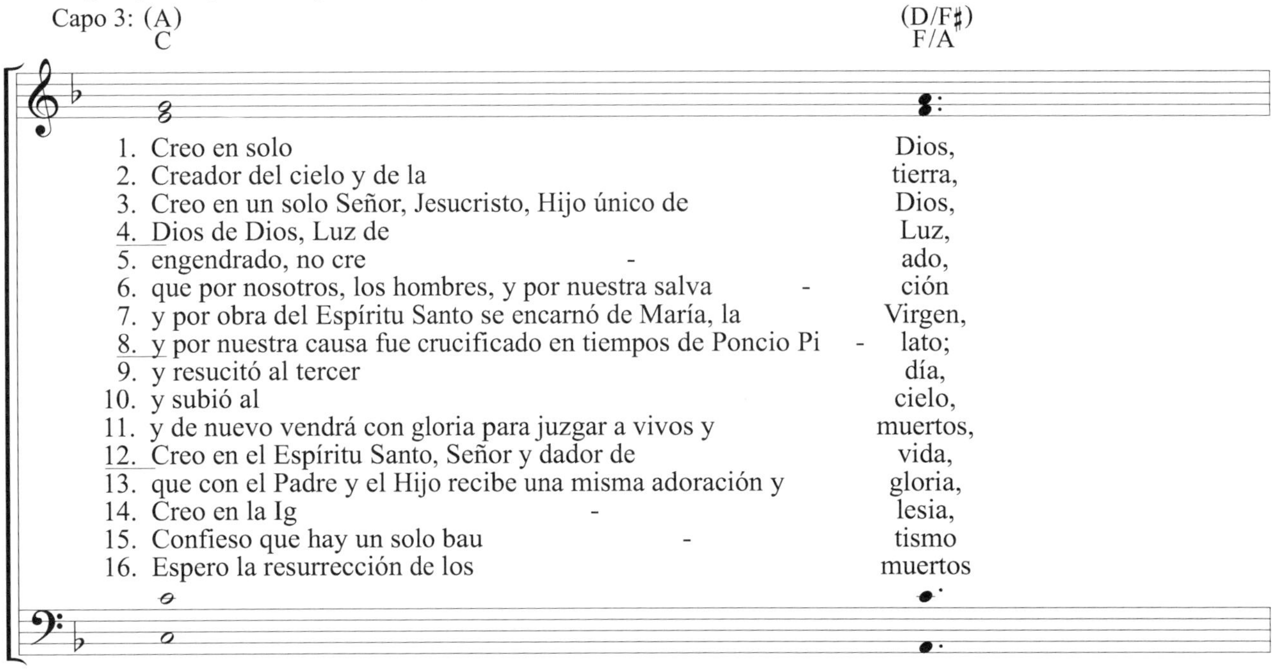


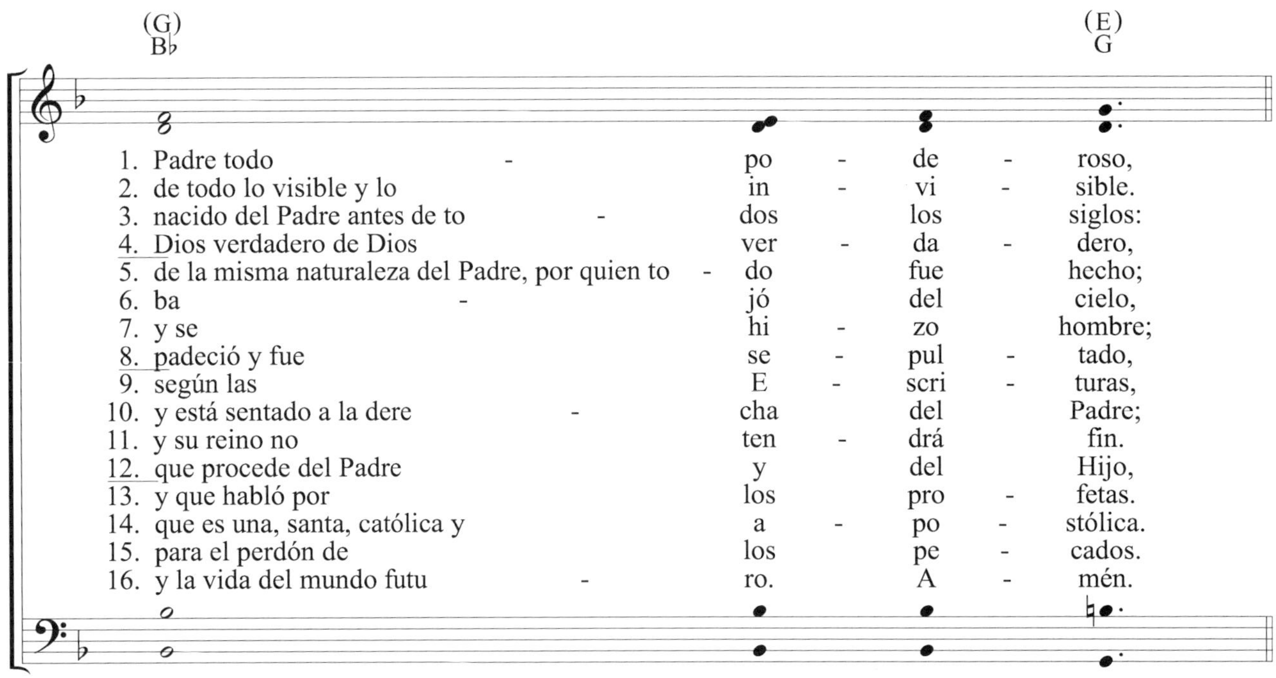


**Performance Notes**

*The chant can be sung with the tenor taking the melody (Setting I), or SATB with the soprano taking the melody (Setting II). The bass descant remains constant whichever version is used.*

*The odd-numbered verses could be sung by a solo cantor and the even-numbered verses by choir and all; or everyone can sing all the verses throughout.*

*Discreet organ accompaniment may be used to sustain the voices. If guitar is used, only one strum per chord symbol should be played.*

# The Lord's Prayer

Latin

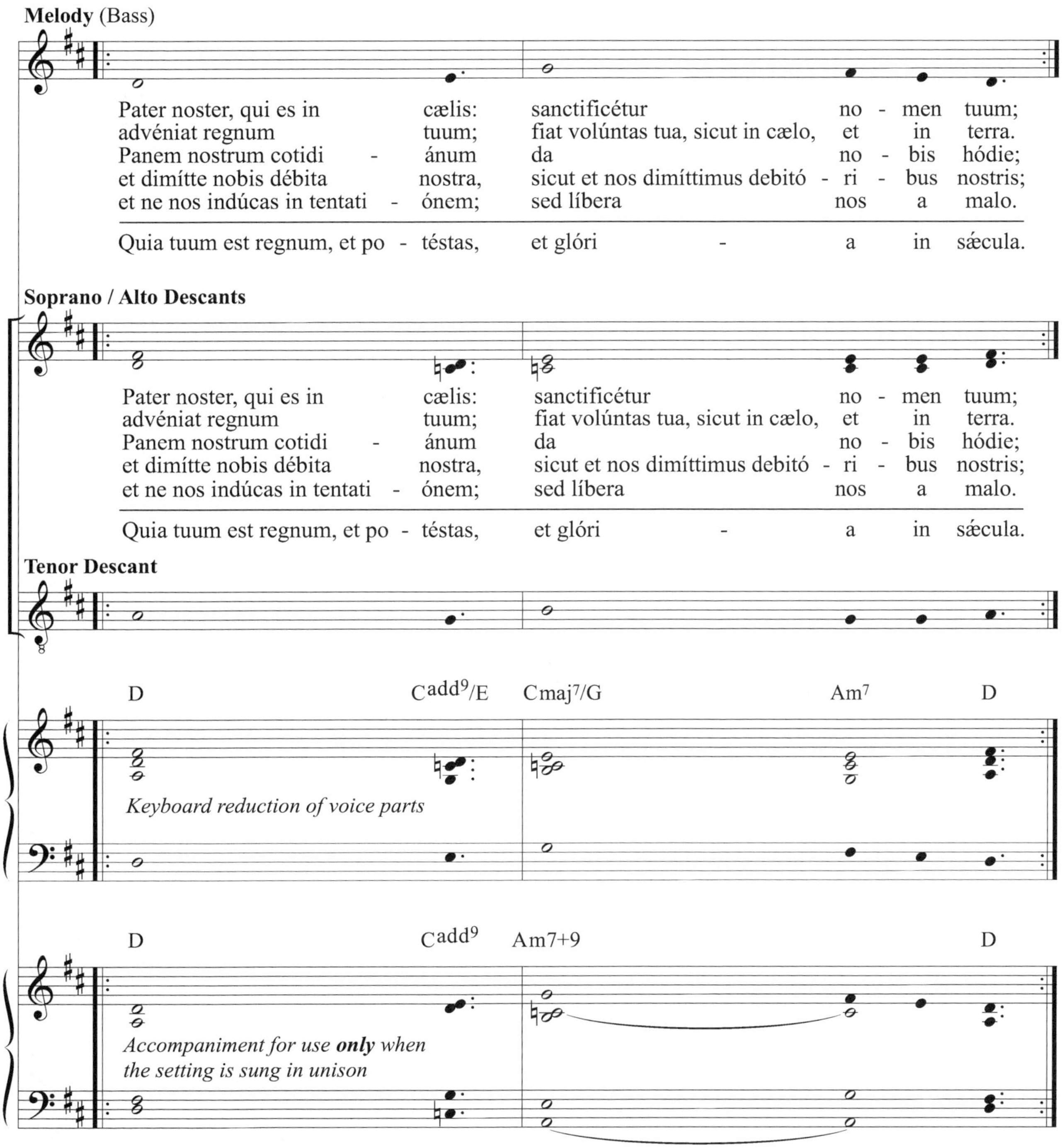


**Performance Notes**

*It is desirable to start this setting with the melody alone (solo voice), then all join in unison at* advéniat regnum tuum. *Add the Tenor descant at* Panem nostrum, the *Alto descant at* et dimítte nobis, *and the Soprano descant at* et ne nos indúcas.

# The Lord's Prayer

English (traditional)

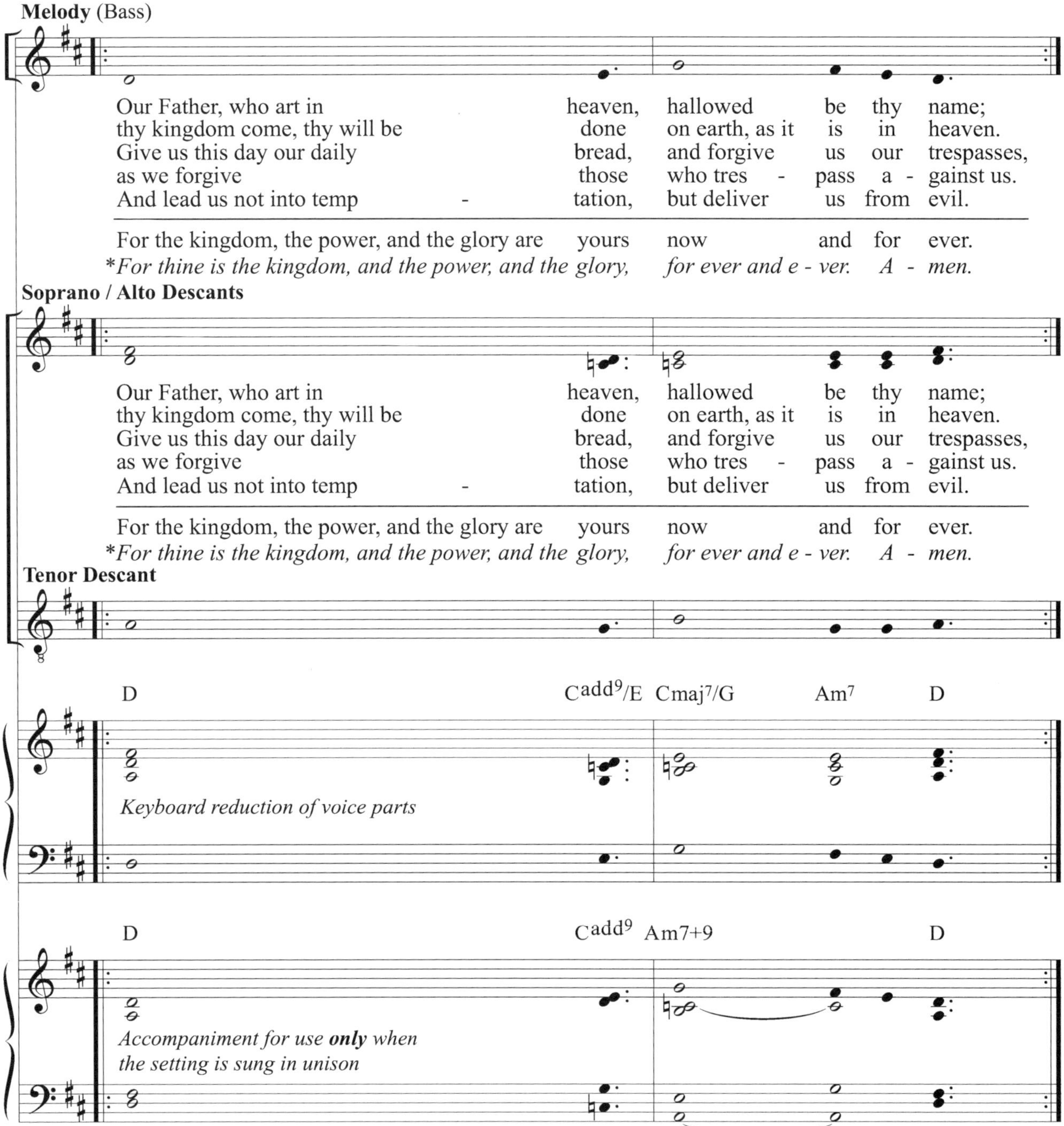


**Performance Notes**

*It is desirable to start this setting with the melody alone (solo voice), then all join in unison at* thy kingdom come. *Add the Tenor descant at* Give us this day, the *Alto descant at* as we forgive, *and the Soprano descant at* And lead us not.

**This version of the Acclamation is for use in Anglican services where the Acclamation text with* Amen *forms an integral part of the Lord's Prayer.*

*A setting of the Lord's Prayer with Embolism is available in the separate collection of music for the Mass written by The Collegeville Composers Group.*

Text: English translation of *The Lord's Prayer* from the 1790 American edition of the *Book of Common Prayer,* adapted from the Anglican *Book of Common Prayer,* 1549.

# The Lord's Prayer

Modern English (ecumenical)

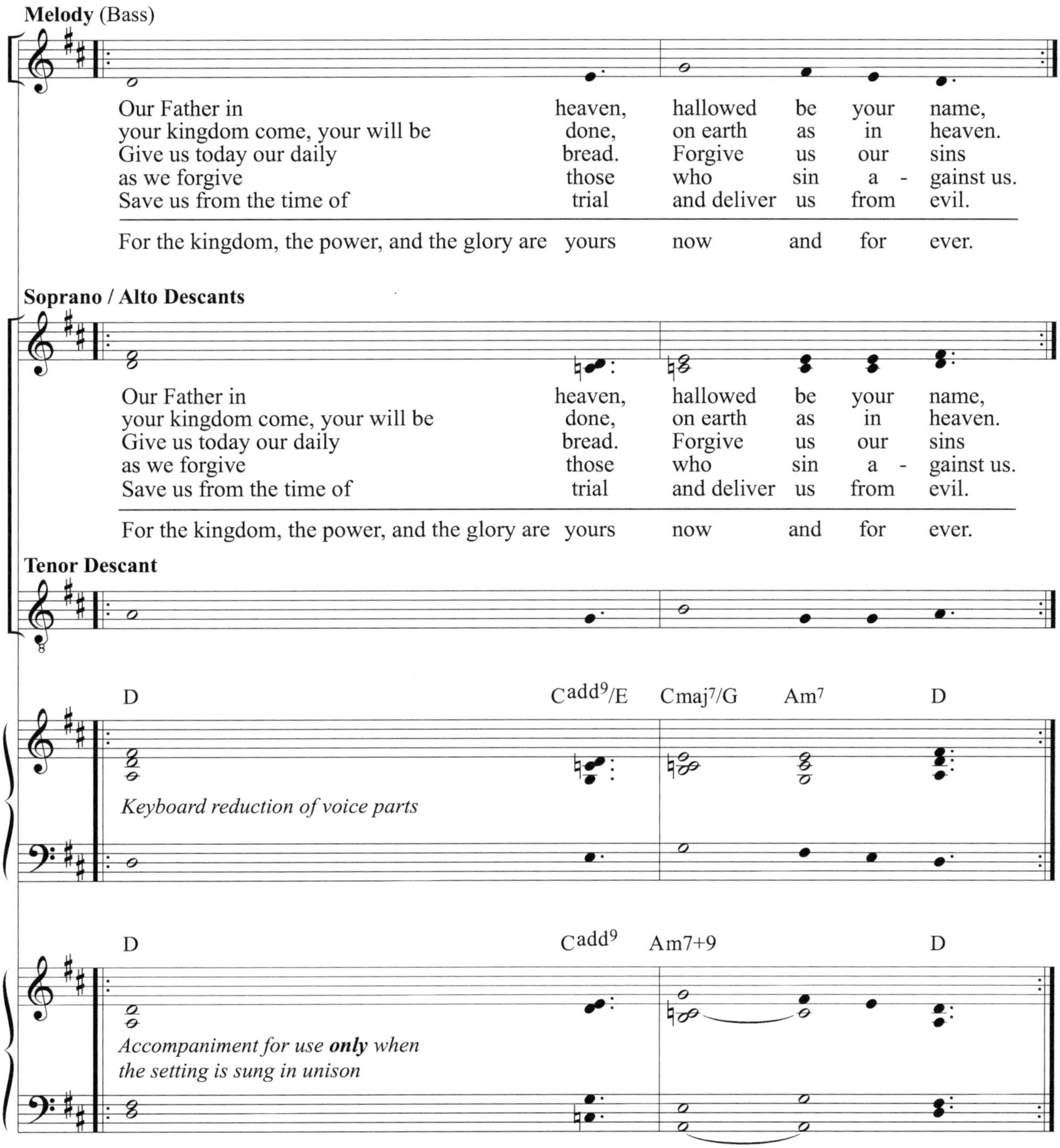


## Performance Notes

*It is desirable to start this setting with the melody alone (solo voice), then all join in unison at* your kingdom come. *Add the Tenor descant at* Give us today, *the Alto descant at* as we forgive, *and the Soprano descant at* Save us from the time.

# The Lord's Prayer

Spanish

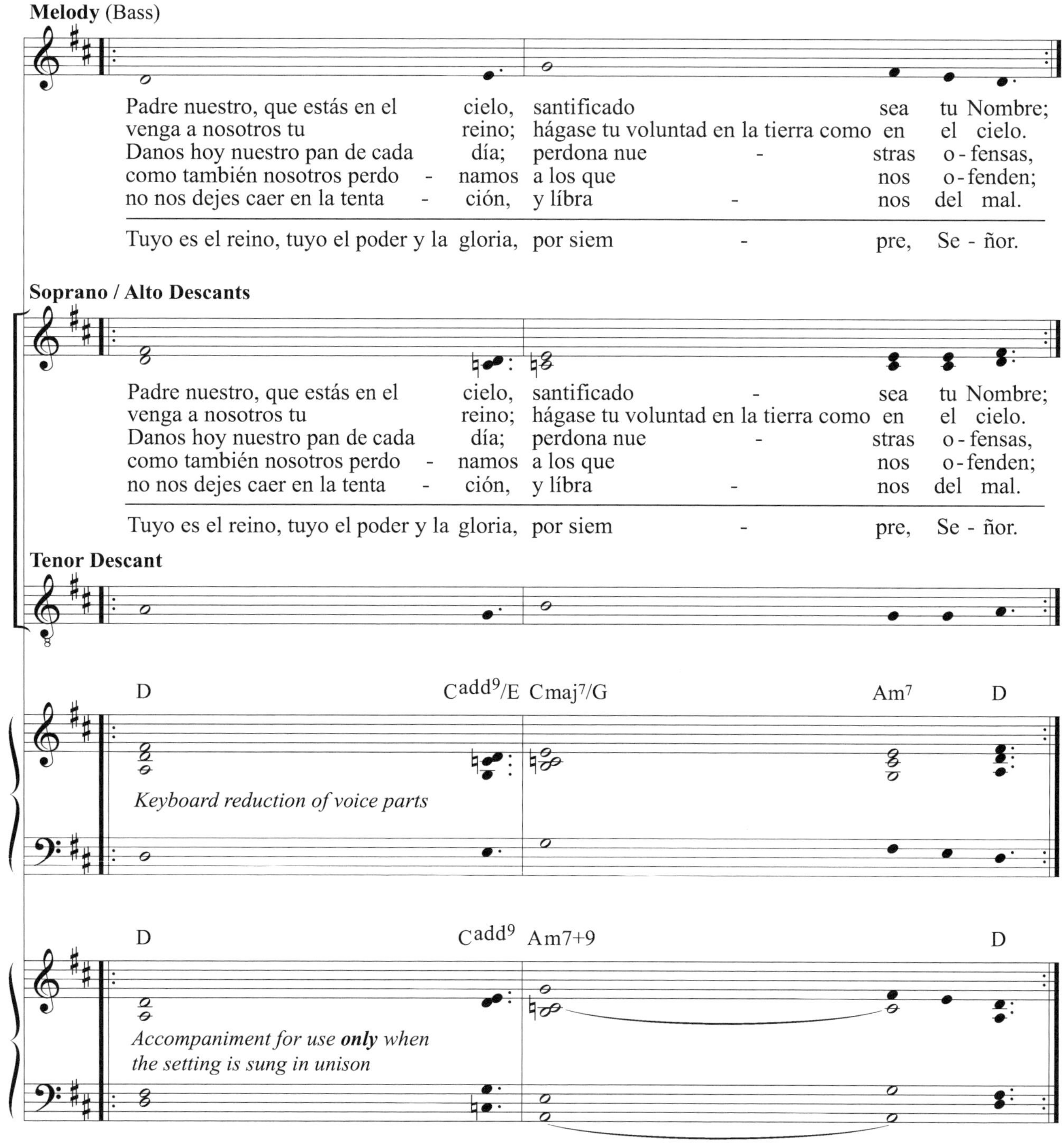


**Performance Notes**

*It is desirable to start this setting with the melody alone (solo voice), then all join in unison at* venga a nosotros. *Add the Tenor descant at* Danos hoy, *the Alto descant at* como también, *and the Soprano descant at* no nos dejes caer.

# The Lord's Prayer

French

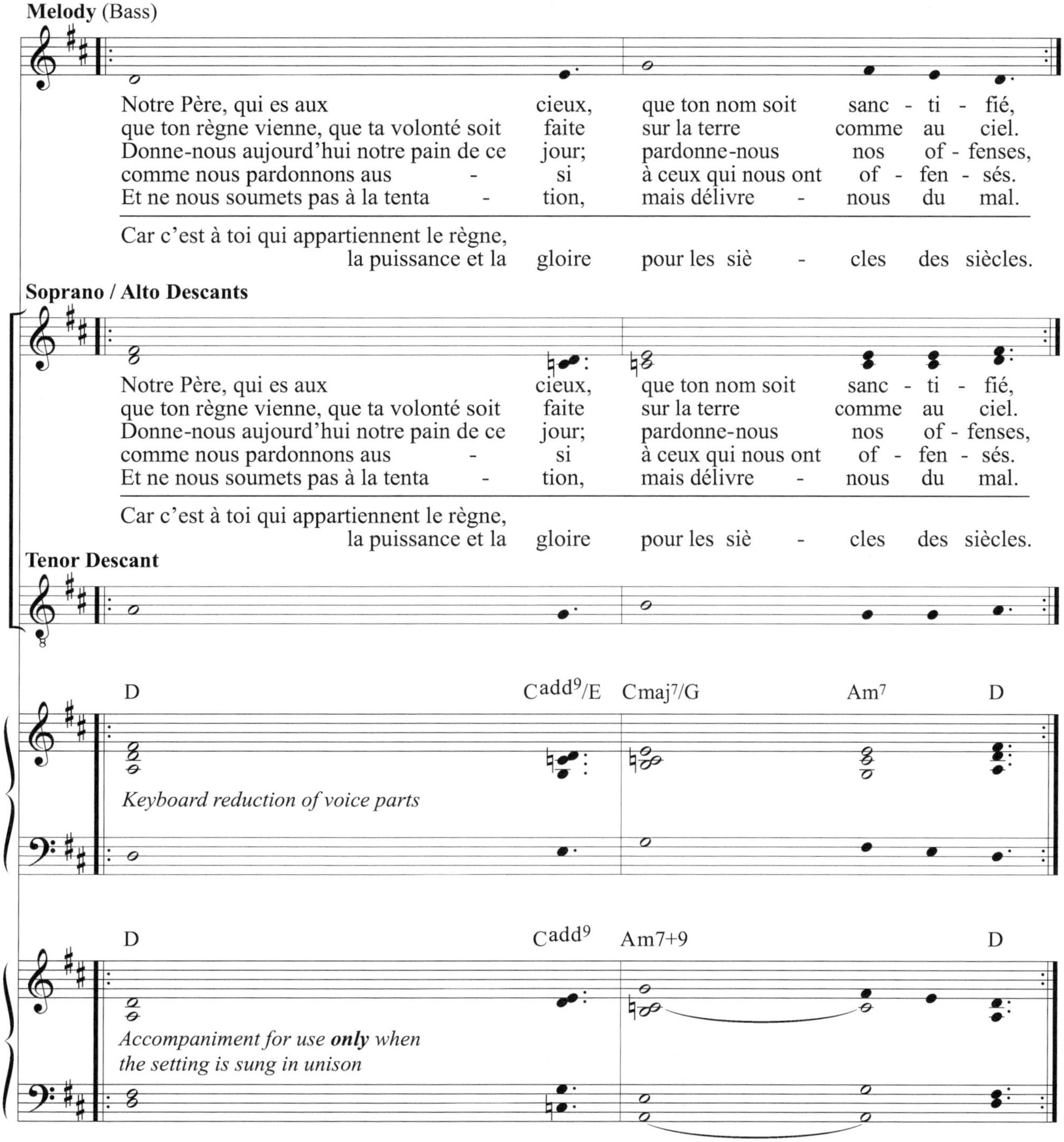


**Performance Notes**

*It is desirable to start this setting with the melody alone (solo voice), then join in unison at* que ton règne vienne. *Add the Tenor descant at* Donne-nous aujourd'hui, *the Alto descant at* comme nous pardonnons *and the Soprano descant at* Et ne nous soumets pas.

Text: Commission mixte Catholique, Orthodoxe, et Protestante, 1964.

# Litany of the Saints

### Opening Dialogue

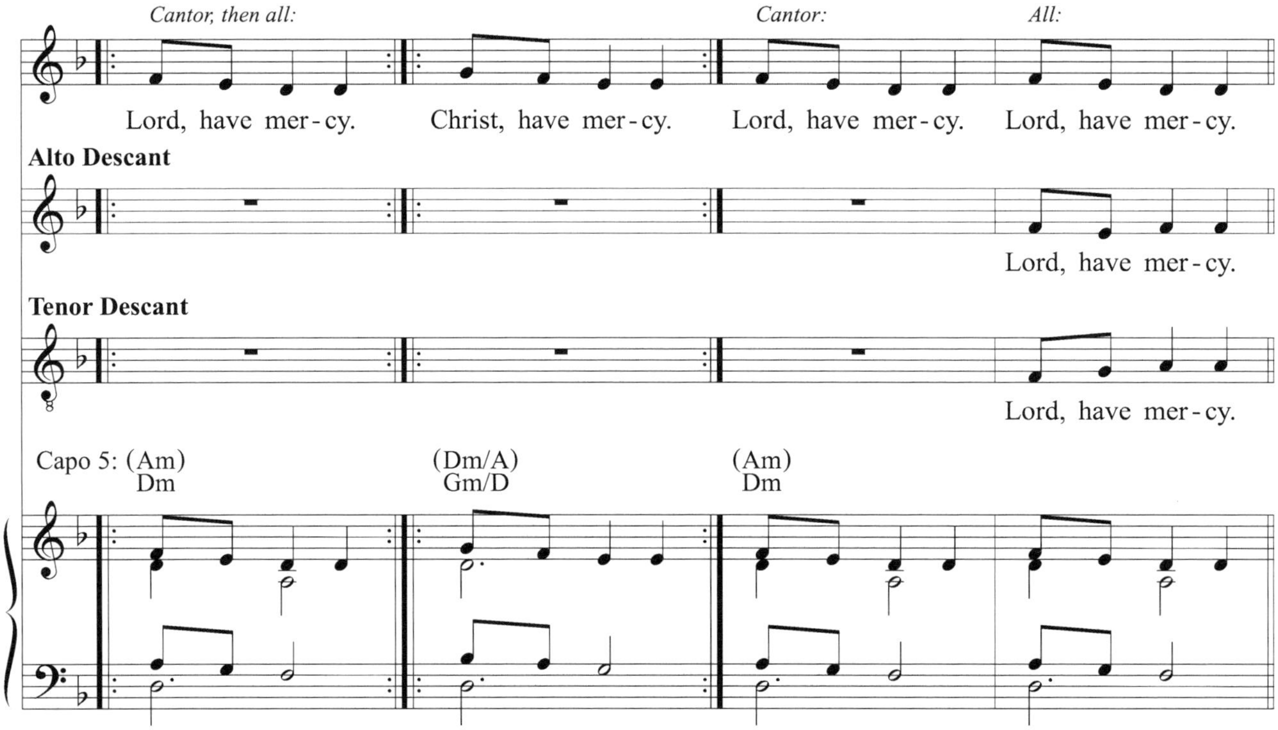


### Alternative Opening Dialogue

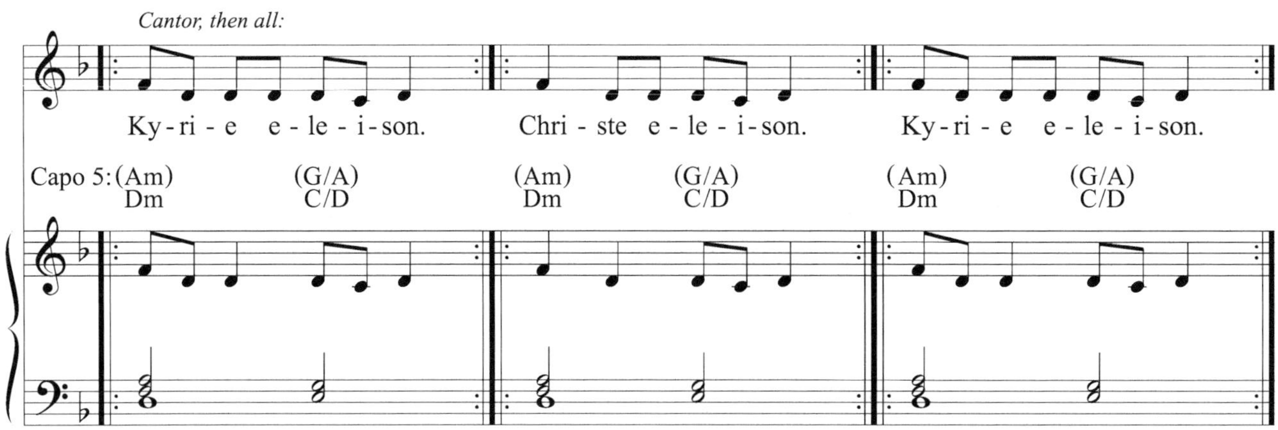

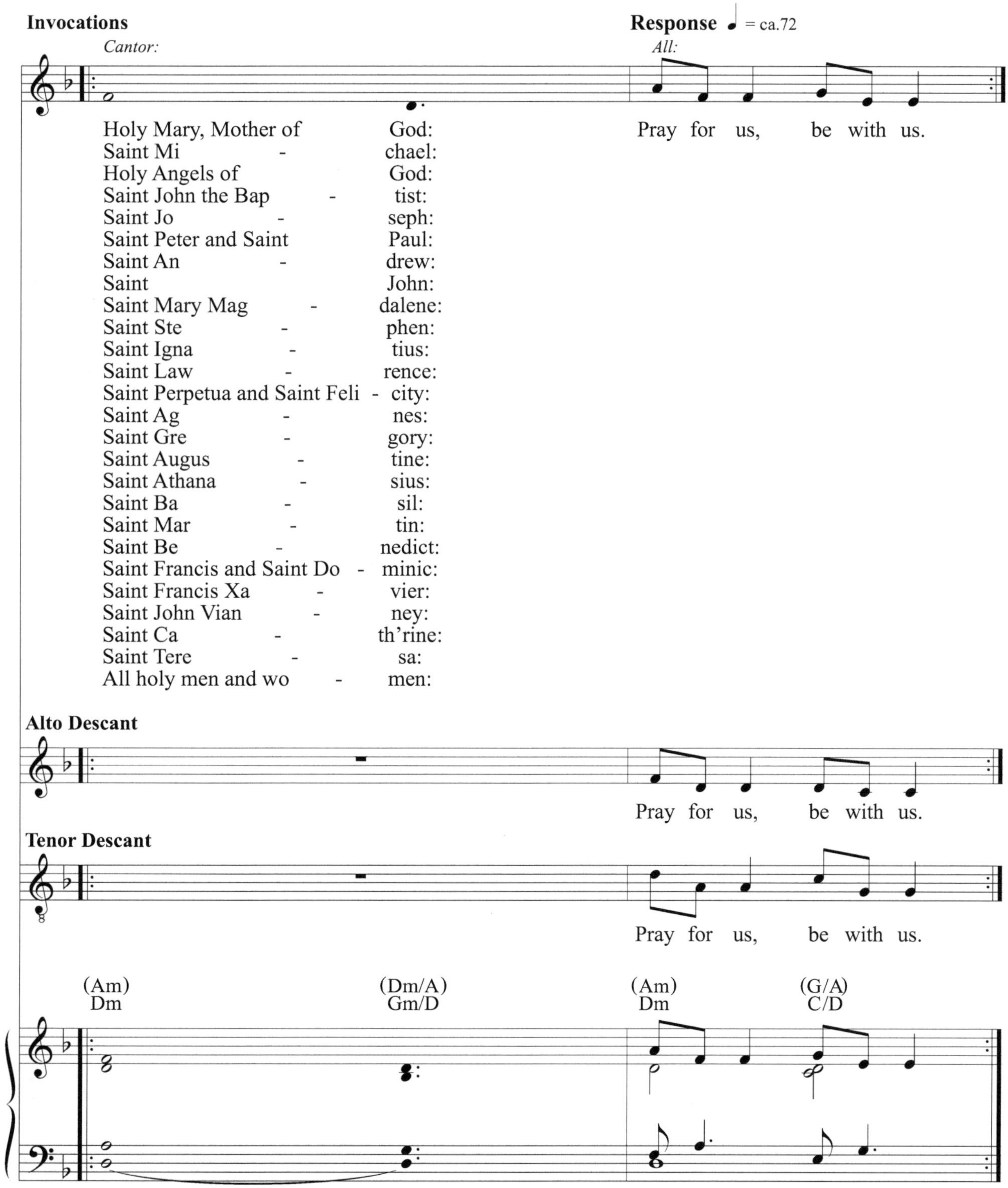
Invocations
Cantor:
Response ♩ = ca.72
All:
Holy Mary, Mother of God:
Saint Mi - chael:
Holy Angels of God:
Saint John the Bap - tist:
Saint Jo - seph:
Saint Peter and Saint Paul:
Saint An - drew:
Saint John:
Saint Mary Mag - dalene:
Saint Ste - phen:
Saint Igna - tius:
Saint Law - rence:
Saint Perpetua and Saint Feli - city:
Saint Ag - nes:
Saint Gre - gory:
Saint Augus - tine:
Saint Athana - sius:
Saint Ba - sil:
Saint Mar - tin:
Saint Be - nedict:
Saint Francis and Saint Do - minic:
Saint Francis Xa - vier:
Saint John Vian - ney:
Saint Ca - th'rine:
Saint Tere - sa:
All holy men and wo - men:
Pray for us, be with us.
Alto Descant
Pray for us, be with us.
Tenor Descant
Pray for us, be with us.
(Am) Dm
(Dm/A) Gm/D
(Am) Dm
(G/A) C/D

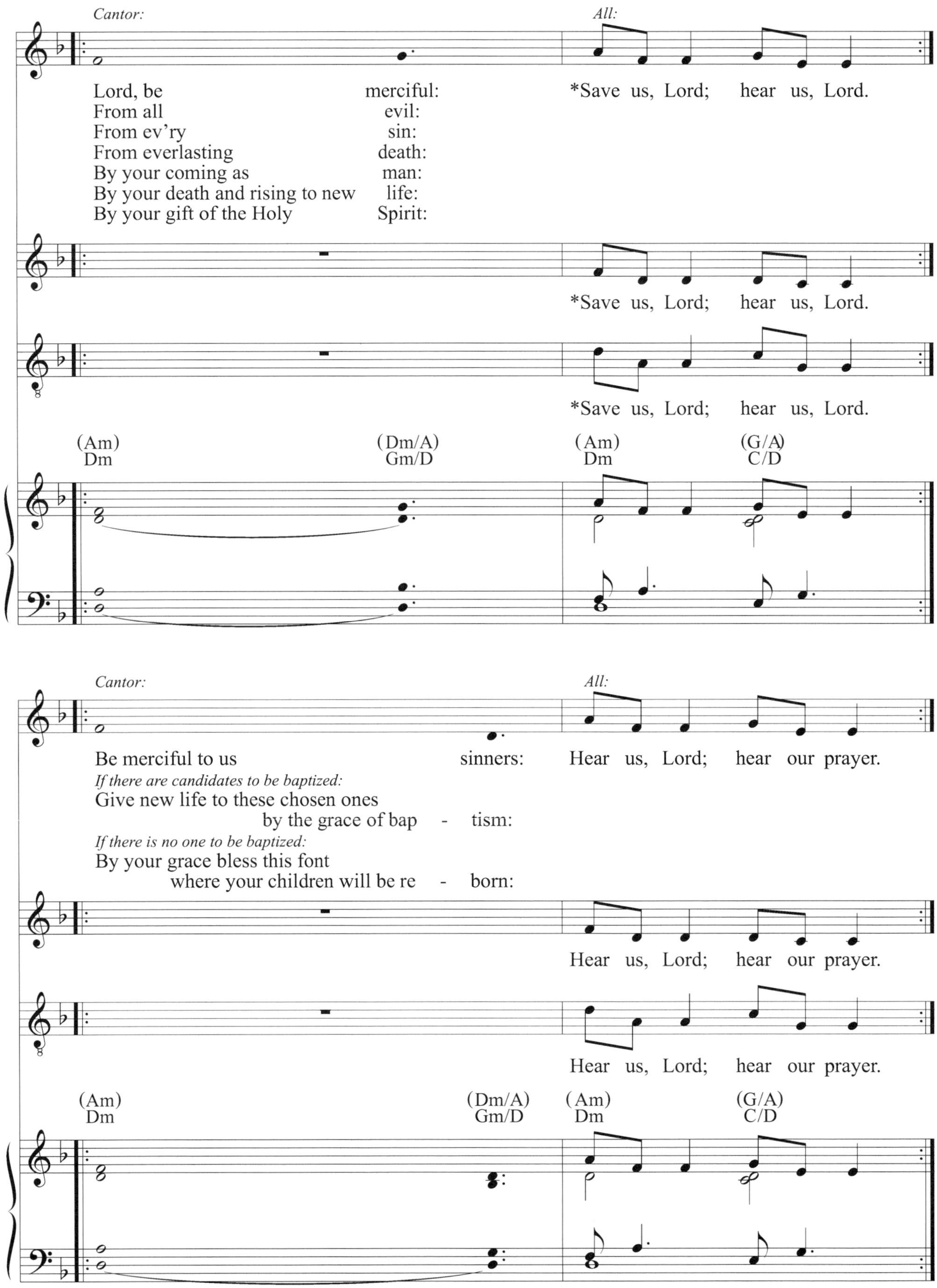
Cantor:
All:
Lord, be merciful: *Save us, Lord; hear us, Lord.
From all evil:
From ev'ry sin:
From everlasting death:
By your coming as man:
By your death and rising to new life:
By your gift of the Holy Spirit:
*Save us, Lord; hear us, Lord.
*Save us, Lord; hear us, Lord.
(Am) Dm
(Dm/A) Gm/D
(Am) Dm
(G/A) C/D
Cantor:
All:
Be merciful to us sinners: Hear us, Lord; hear our prayer.
If there are candidates to be baptized:
Give new life to these chosen ones
by the grace of bap - tism:
If there is no one to be baptized:
By your grace bless this font
where your children will be re - born:
Hear us, Lord; hear our prayer.
Hear us, Lord; hear our prayer.
(Am) Dm
(Dm/A) Gm/D
(Am) Dm
(G/A) C/D

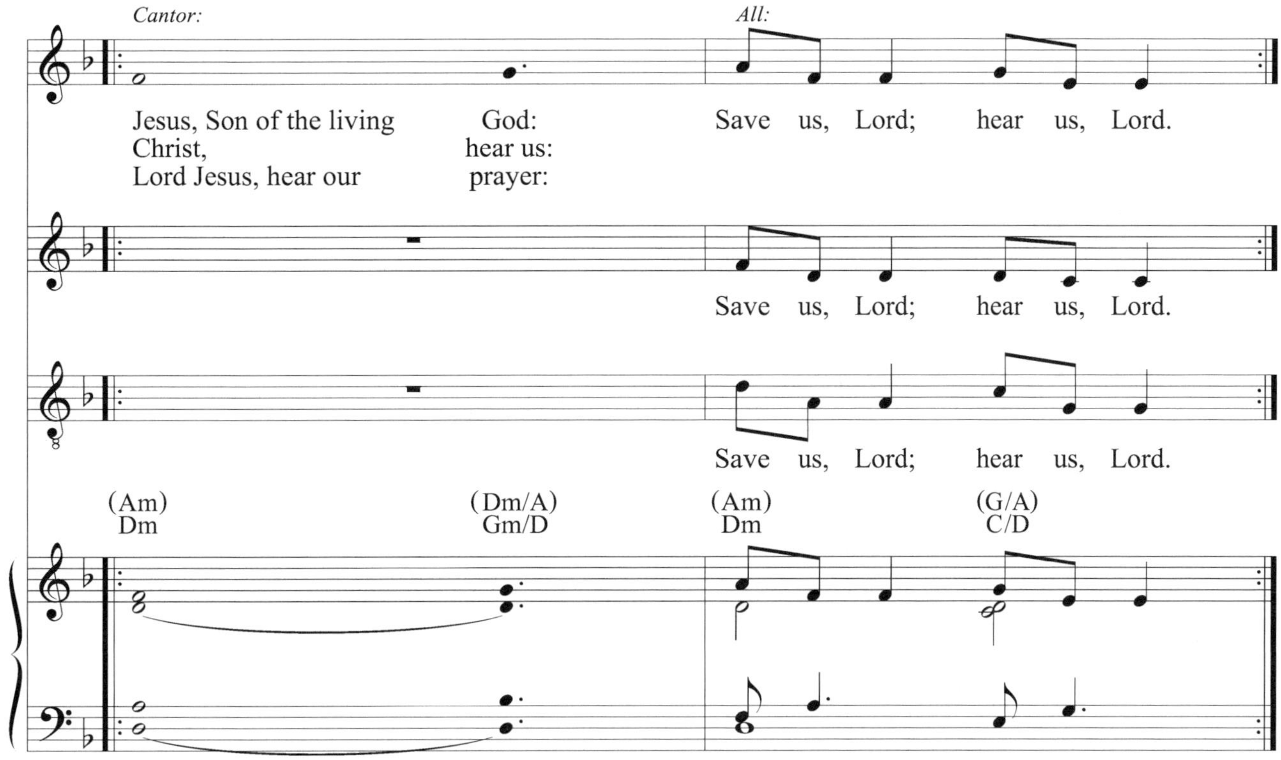


**Performance Notes**

**The various sections may be differentiated in the traditional manner by the use of a different response; or, if desired, all the sections from here to the end of the Litany could use the* Lord, be merciful *response instead of changing the response for each section.*

*The accompaniment is entirely optional. Ideally, this Litany should be sung* a cappella. *Keep the music moving to enhance its dialogic nature. A slight rallentando on the final response and a fermata on the last unresolved chord will leave the way open for prayer to continue.*

*In the Litany, some names of saints may be added, especially the titular of the church, the local patrons, or the saints of those to be baptized.*

*The section in the lower half of page 36 may have additional intercessions added to it, for example, naming in a separate intercession each individual who is to be baptized.*

# Praise to You, Alleluia

Blessing and Invocation of God over the Baptismal Water

**Blessing and Invocation**

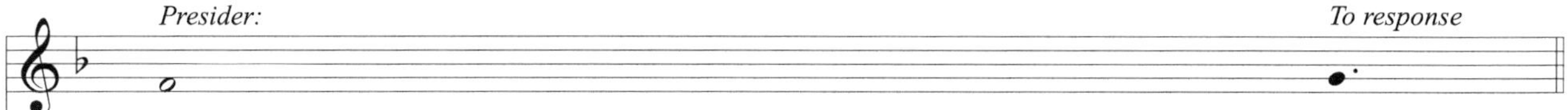


1. Praise to you, almighty God and Father,
   for you have created water to cleanse and give life.
2. Praise to you, Lord Jesus Christ, the Father's only Son,
   for you offered yourself on the cross,
3. that in the blood and water flowing from your side
   and through your death and resurrection the Church might be born.
4. Praise to you, God the Holy Spirit,
   for you anointed Christ at his baptism in the waters of the Jordan,
   that we might all be baptized in you.
5. Come to us, Lord, Father of all,
   and make holy this water which you have cre - ated,
6. so that all who are baptized in it may be washed clean of sin
   and be born again to live as your children.
7. Make this water holy, Lord,
   so that all who are baptized into Christ's death and resurrection by this water
   may become more perfectly like your Son.

*If there is water to be blessed, the presider touches the water with his right hand and continues with verse 8:*
*OR*
*During the Easter season, if the water has already been blessed, verse 8 is omitted and the presider concludes with the spoken* Concluding Prayer *on the next page.*

**Response** (♩ = ca. 92)

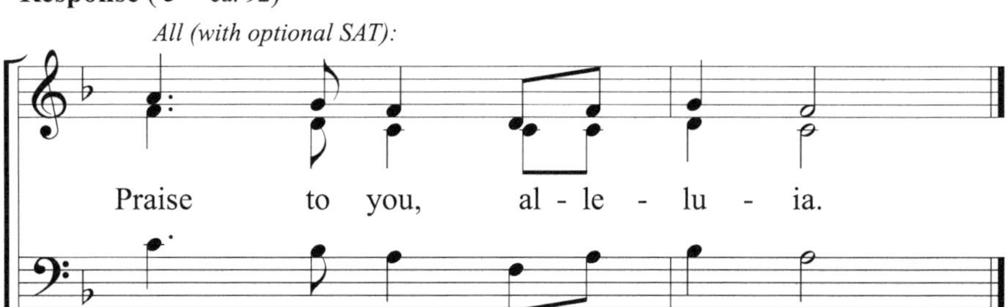


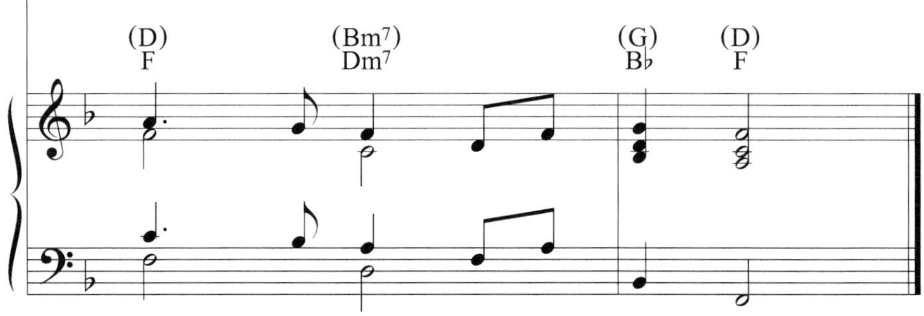

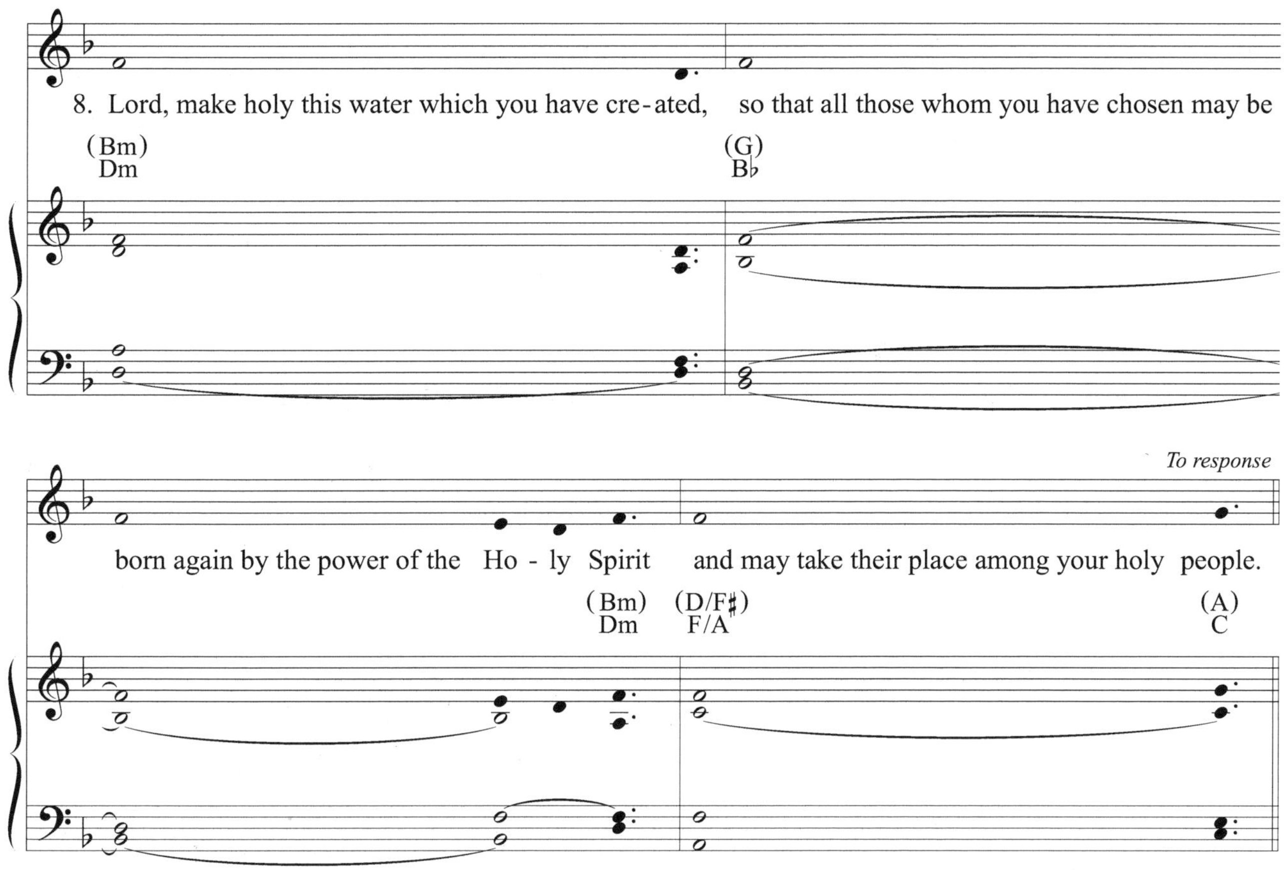


**Concluding Prayer**

**Presider:** You have called your children, *N.* and *N.*, to this cleansing water,
that they may share in the faith of your Church and have eternal life.
By the mystery of this consecrated water
lead them to a new and spiritual birth.
We ask this through Christ our Lord.

**All:** Amen.

**Performance Notes**
*This litany form could be adapted for use with many other texts.*

# One Lord, One Hope, One Faith We Proclaim

Infant and Adult Baptism Song / Profession of Faith

God who is all in all.
God who is all in all.
(A) D
(G) C
(Fmaj7) B♭maj7
(G) C
(A) D

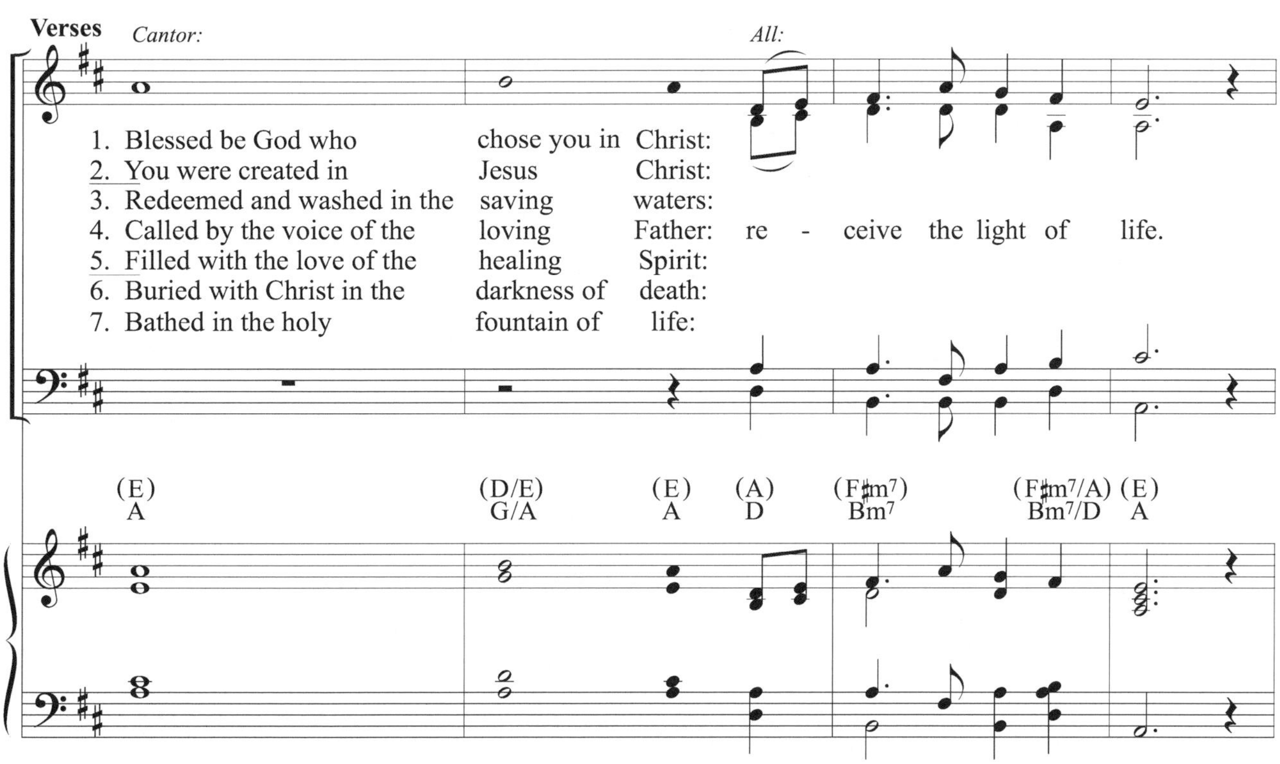
Verses
Cantor:
All:
1. Blessed be God who chose you in Christ:
2. You were created in Jesus Christ:
3. Redeemed and washed in the saving waters:
4. Called by the voice of the loving Father:
5. Filled with the love of the healing Spirit:
6. Buried with Christ in the darkness of death:
7. Bathed in the holy fountain of life:
re - ceive the light of life.
(E) A
(D/E) G/A
(E) A
(A) D
(F♯m7) Bm7
(F♯m7/A) Bm7/D
(E) A

**Performance Notes**

*The notation for the verses is very approximate. They may be chanted in free speech rhythm, or sung in a more metrical fashion.*

*The verses incorporate a mosaic of scriptural reminiscences:*

*Verse 1* Ephesians 1:3-4; Ephesians 2:10
*Verse 2* Ephesians 2:10; Ephesians 5:1-2 and Galatians 6:2
*Verse 3* 1 Corinthians 6:11; Ephesians 1:18
*Verse 4* Matthew 3:17; 2 Thessalonians 2:14
*Verse 5* Ephesians 1:13; Revelation 7:17
*Verse 6* Colossians 2:12; Titus 3:5 and Galatians 2:16
*Verse 7* Psalm 35:9; 2 Thessalonians 1:5

# You Will Be My Witnesses

Rite of Confirmation: Song for the Word

**Verses** *Psalm 22:23-24ab, 26-27, 28, 31-32*

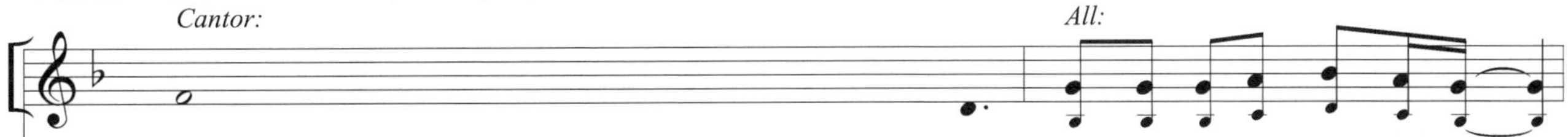


1. I will tell of your name to my people; when the Spi-rit comes to you.
2. "You who fear the LORD give praise;
3. You are my praise in the great as - sembly;
4. The poor shall eat and have their fill;
5. May their hearts live;
6. All the earth shall remember and return to the LORD;
7. My children too shall serve;
8. They shall declare to those unborn, the faithfulness of God;

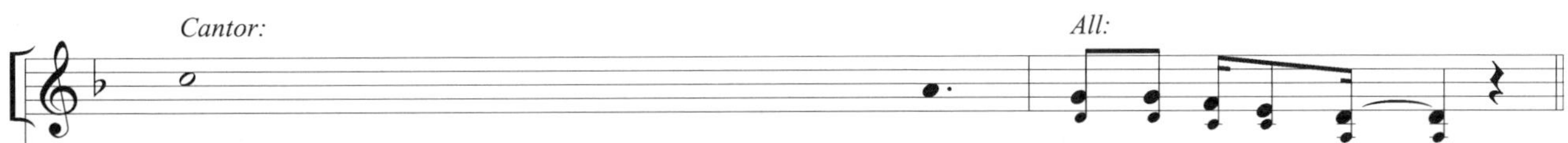


1. and praise you where they are as - sembled; when the Spi-rit comes.
2. all children of Jacob, give glory;"
3. My vows I will pay before those who fear God;
4. Those who seek the LORD shall praise the LORD;
5. for ever and ever!
6. all families of the nations shall bow down in awe;
7. They shall tell of the LORD to generations yet to come;
8. "These things the LORD has done;"

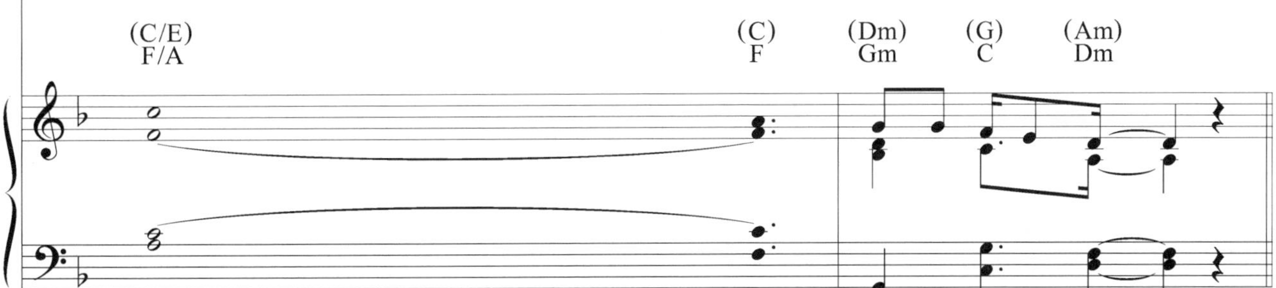

# Taste the Goodness of the Word of God

Rite of Confirmation: Song for the Table

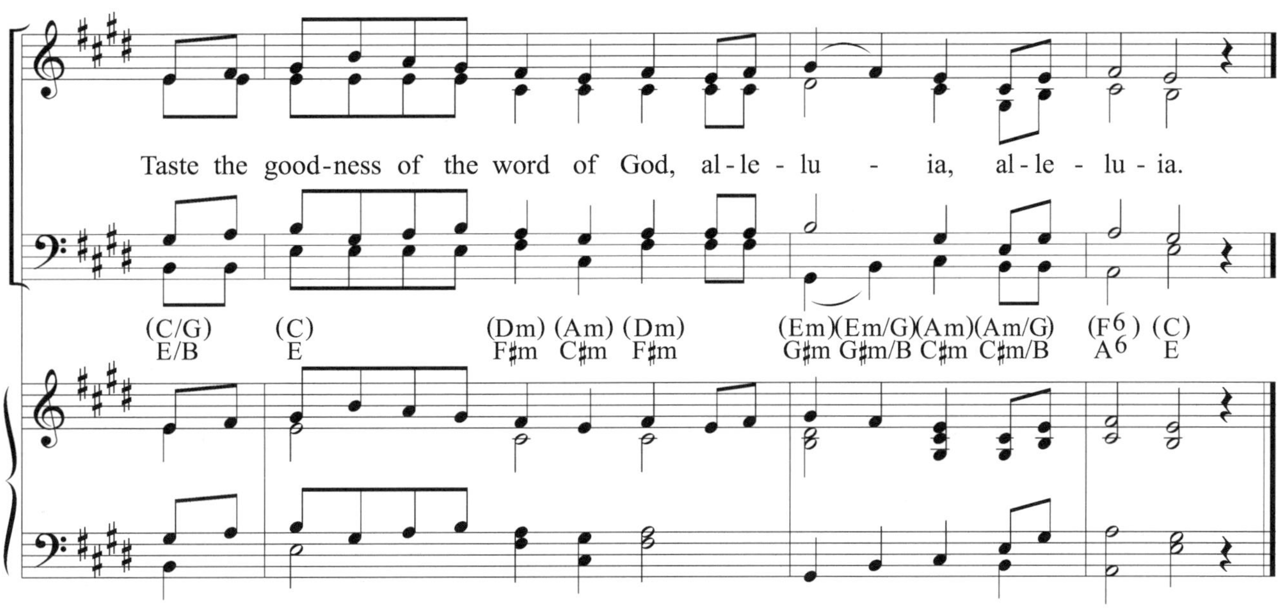


**Verses** *Hebrews 4:12, 16; 6:19, 20; 2:9b, 14-15, 17ab+18; Psalm 95:1-9*

| | | | |
|---|---|---|---|
| 1. | The word of God is living | and | active, |
| 2. | Let us approach the throne of grace | with | boldness, |
| 3. | We have | this | hope, |
| 4. | where Jesus, a forerunner on our behalf, | has | entered, |
| 5. | Jesus for a little while was made lower than | the | angels, |
| 6. | Since the children whom God has given Jesus share flesh | and | blood, |
| 7. | Therefore he had to become like his brothers and sisters in every | re - | spect, |
| 8. | Come, ring out our joy to | the | LORD; |
| 9. | A mighty God is the LORD, a great king a - | bove | all gods, |
| 10. | Come in; let us bow and | bend | low; |
| 11. | O that today you would listen to | God's | voice! |

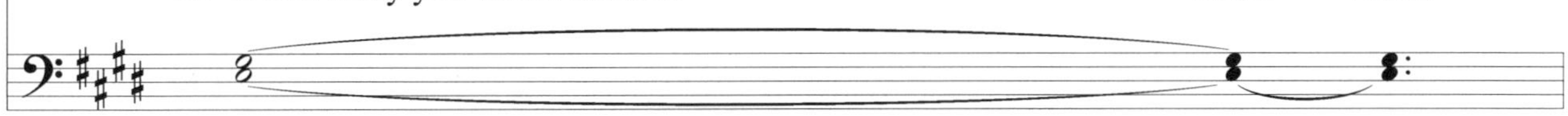

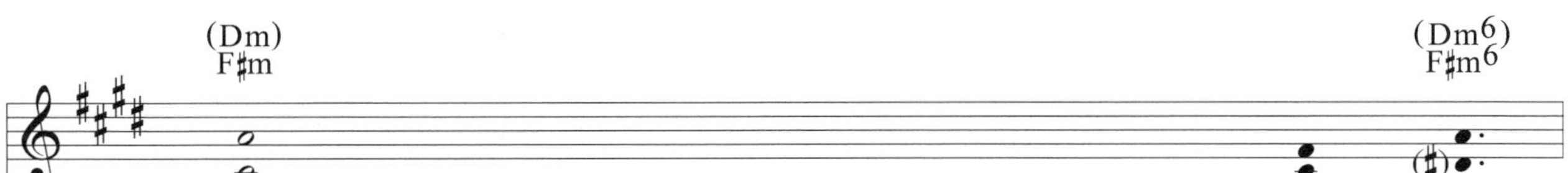


| | | | |
|---|---|---|---|
| 1. | sharper than any two - | edged | sword, |
| 2. | so that we may re - | ceive | mercy |
| 3. | a sure and steadfast anchor of | the | soul, |
| 4. | having become a high priest | for | ever |
| 5. | but is now crowned with glory and honor because of the suffering | of | death, |
| 6. | he himself likewise shared | the | same things, |
| 7. | so that he might be a merciful and faithful high priest in the service | of | God. |
| 8. | hail the rock | who | saves us. |
| 9. | in whose hands are the depths of the earth; the heights of the mountains | as | well. |
| 10. | let us kneel before the God | who | made us |
| 11. | "Harden not your hearts as at | Me - | ribah, |

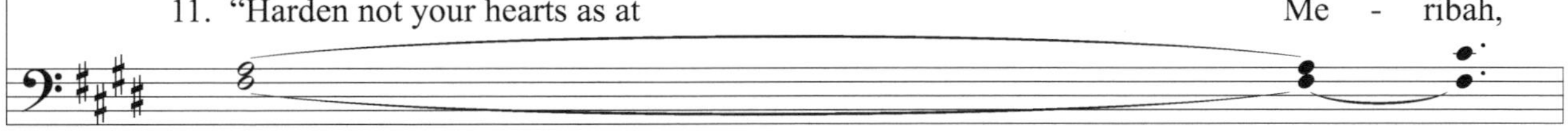

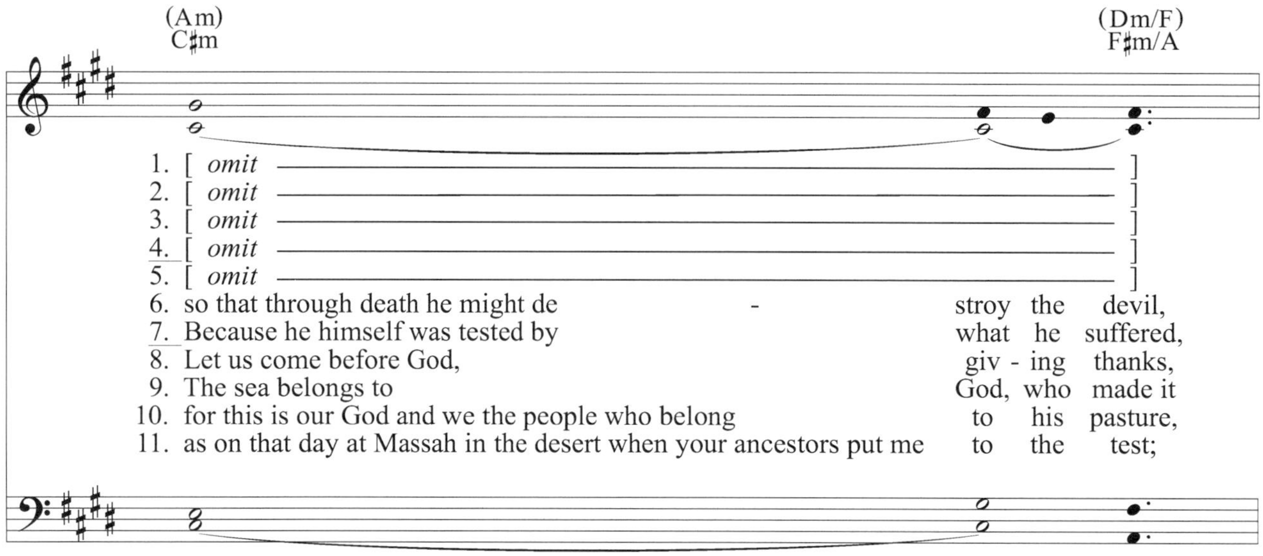


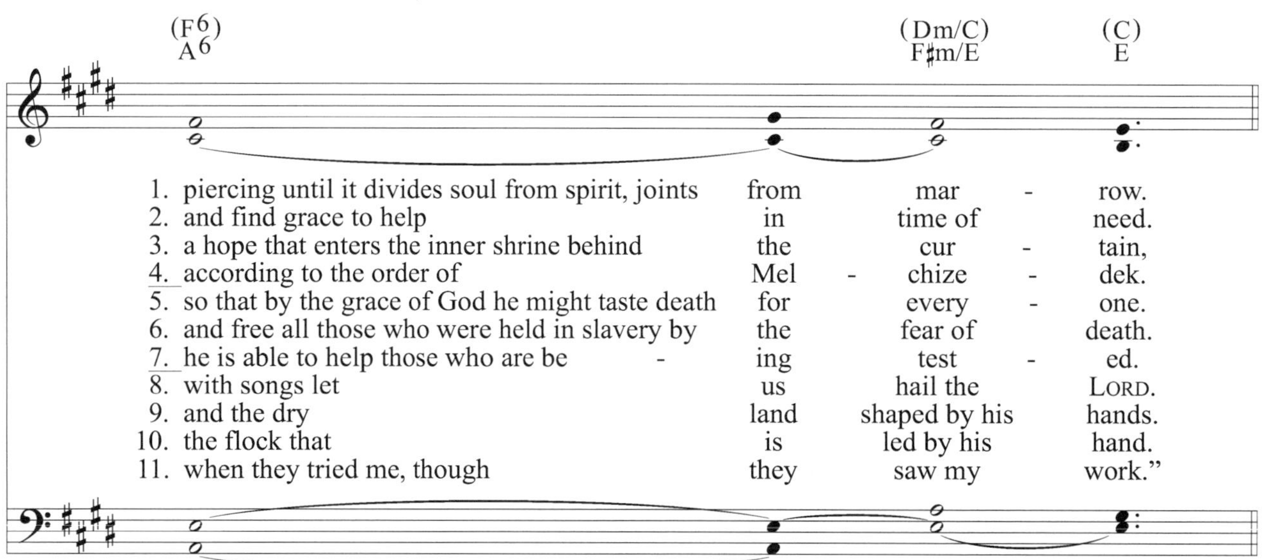


**Performance Notes**

*The Antiphon may also be used as a stand-alone refrain without verses. The 5/4 measures at the end of each system of the antiphon are deliberate, the rest giving breathing-space between phrases.*

# Lord, We Praise You

Rite of Acceptance into the Order of Catechumens:
Affirmation by the Sponsors and the Assembly
(Presider)

**Invocations**

*Presider:*

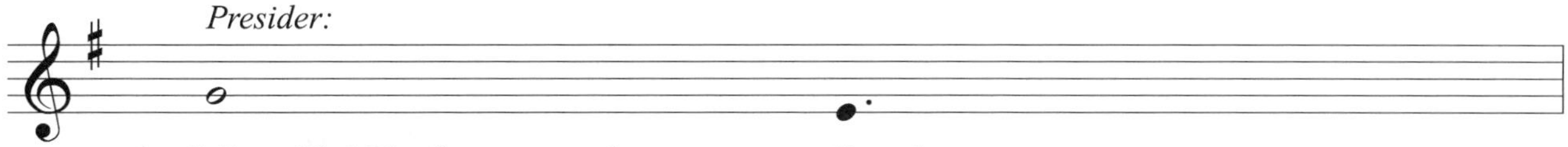

**1. Merciful Father, we give you thanks**
**2. In love you looked for them,**
**3. They have turned from their paths**
**4. Now they have spoken,**
**5. Great is our joy**

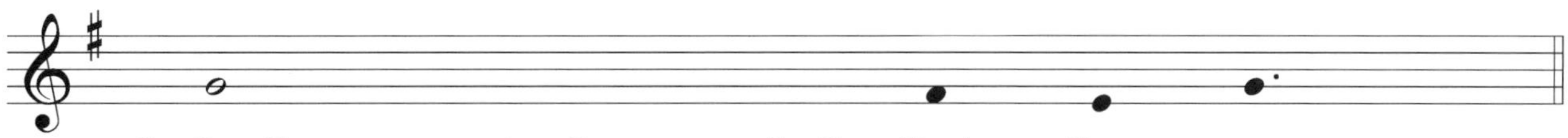

**1. for these servants of yours and all that they are:**
**2. in different ways you called them:**
**3. to seek you and know you:**
**4. now we have heard them:**
**5. as we wel - come them here:**

**Response** *All:*

Lord, we praise you; Lord, we bless you.

# We Adore You, O Christ, and We Praise You

Rite of Acceptance into the Order of Catechumens:
Signing of the Senses
(Presider)

**Verse 1**

*Presider: (as each sense is signed by him or another minister)*

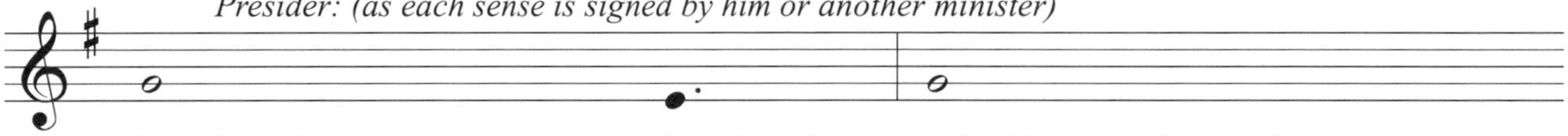

**1. Receive the cross on your forehead. It is Christ himself who now**

**1. strengthens you with this sign of his love. Learn to know and fol-low him.**

**Refrain**

*All:*

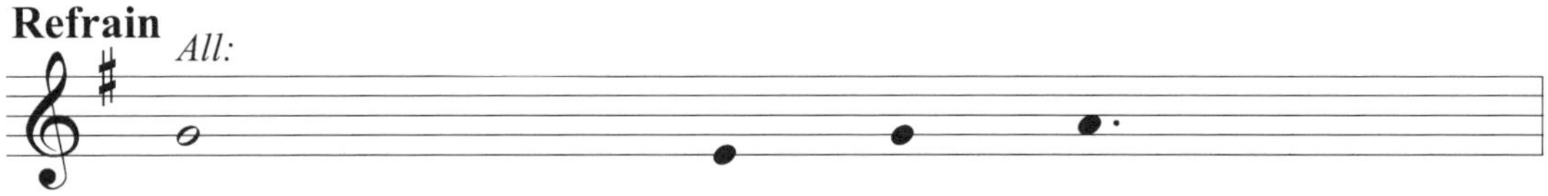

We adore you, O Christ, and we praise you:

*To additional verses or Final Blessing*

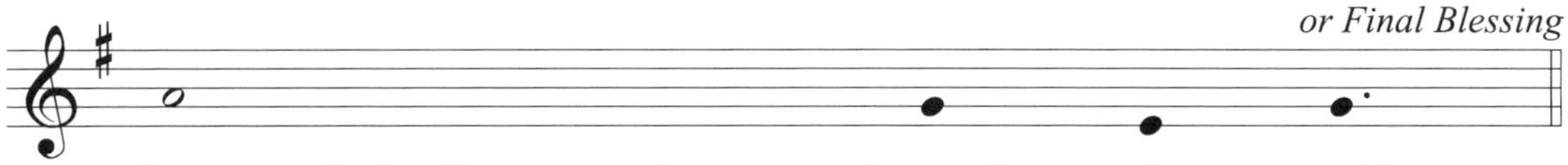

by your holy Cross you have re - deemed the world.

**Verses 2–8**

*Presider: (these verses are optional in the rite, or a selection of them may be chosen)*

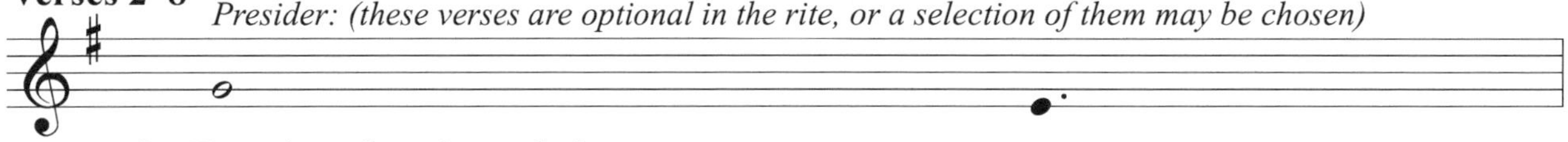

**2. Receive the sign of the cross on your ears,**
**3. Receive the sign of the cross on your eyes,**
**4. Receive the sign of the cross on your lips,**
**5. Receive the sign of the cross over your heart,**
**6. Receive the sign of the cross on your shoulders,**
**7. Receive the sign of the cross on your hands,**
**8. Receive the sign of the cross on your feet,**

*To refrain*

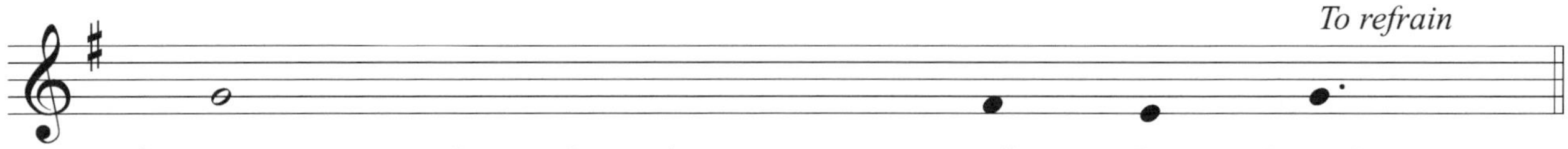

**2. that you may hear the voice of the Lord.**
**3. that you may see the glo - ry of God.**
**4. that you may respond to the word of God.**
**5. that Christ may dwell there by faith.**
**6. that you may bear the gentle yoke of Christ.**
**7. that Christ may be known in the work that you do.**
**8. that you may walk in the way of Christ.**

**Final Blessing**

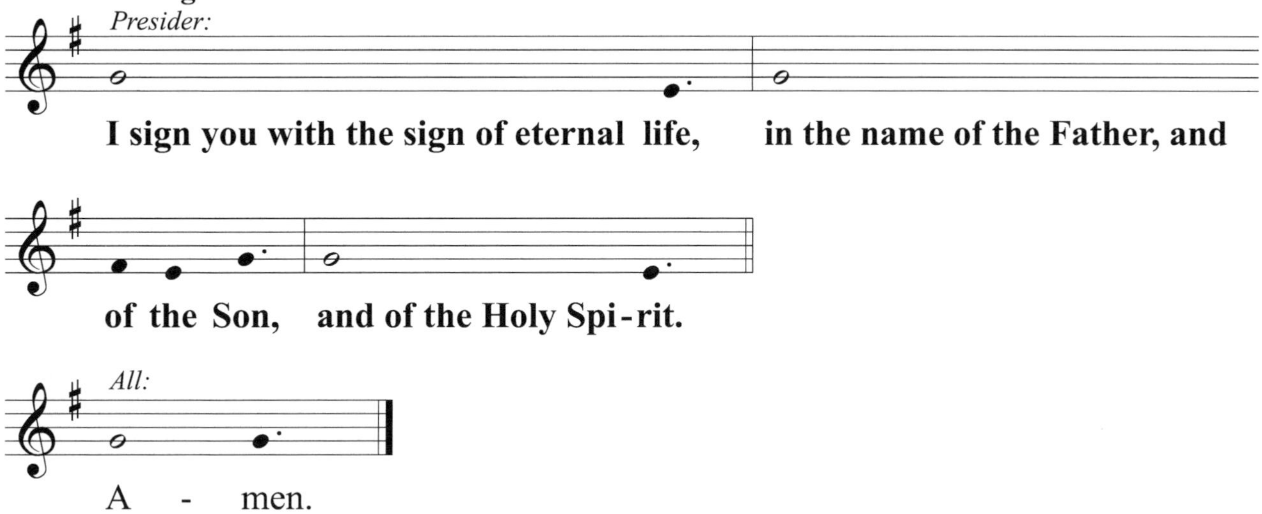


**Performance Notes**

*After the senses have been signed, the presider alone may make the sign of the cross over all the candidates at once, without touching them, and singing the blessing. If there are more than two or three candidates and the decision is taken to bless them individually instead of collectively, it may be preferable for the blessing to be spoken rather than sung.*

# Go in Peace

Rite of Christian Initiation of Adults:
Dismissal of the Catechumens
(Presider)

**Invocations**

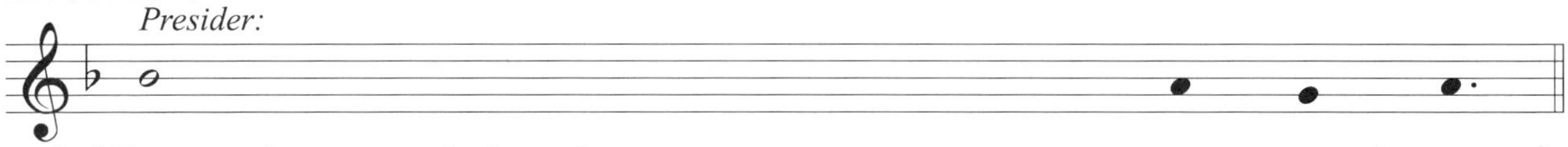


**1. {Go now in peace, beloved ca - te - chumens.**
***or* Go now in peace, be - lov - ed friends.}**
**2. May the Lord's peace remain with you always.**
**3. Feed on God's word, and grow in God's strength.**
**4. One day, we pray, you will share the Lord's table.**

*Additional invocations during Lent and other times*

**5. May God create a pure heart in you and give you help.**
**6. May you be nourished not on bread alone but on every word from God.**
**7. May you be the beloved of the Lord, and rejoice in his favor.**
**8. May the Lord, the savior of the world, give you the liv - ing water.**
**9. Follow the light of the world and have the light of life.**
**10. Believe in Jesus, the resurrection and the life.**
**11. Believe in God's only Son and have e - ter - nal life.**
**12. May you follow the Lord and re - joice in serving him.**
**13. Repent, for the kingdom of heaven is close at hand.**
**14. Acknowledge your sins, and find joy in God's mercy.**
**15. Seek good and not evil, and the God of hosts will be with you.**
**16. Listen always to the voice of the Lord.**
**17. Be open to a heart and a spirit that are new.**
**18. Count on God's mercy and fullness of re - demption.**
**19. Be noble and generous,**
**and yield a harvest through your per - se - verance.**

**Response**

**Additional Invocations** (general use)

*Presider:*

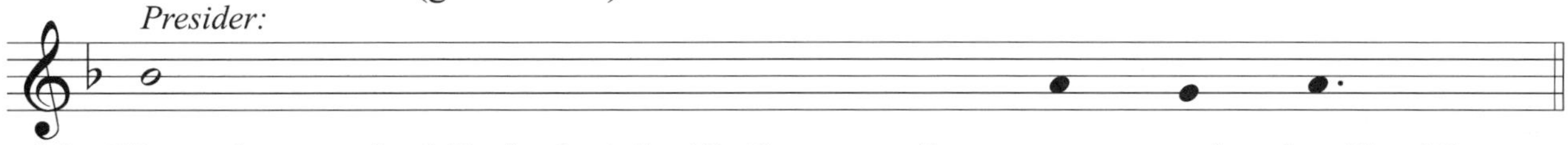

**20. Keep the word of God, that the Father may love you and dwell with you.**
**21. May God make you holy in the truth.**
**22. May your heart(s) be open to hear the words of God's Son.**
**23. May the Father of our Lord Jesus Christ enlighten the eyes of your mind.**
**24. Stay awake and stand ready!**
**25. Keep faithful, that you may receive the crown of life.**

**Response**

*All:*

Go in peace, go in peace.

**Performance Notes**

*Verses 1–4 are for general use, derived from the rite itself. Others may be selected from those given above, derived from the Sunday Gospel Acclamations for Lent and Ordinary Time, or you can write your own. Use as many verses as necessary to cover the departure of the catechumens - four verses would be a good minimum.*
*This setting can also be used as a recessional song at the end of Mass, following the dismissal by the deacon/priest, as well as at other blessing occasions.*

# Praise to You, Alleluia

Blessing and Invocation of God over the Baptismal Water
(Presider)

**Blessing and Invocation**

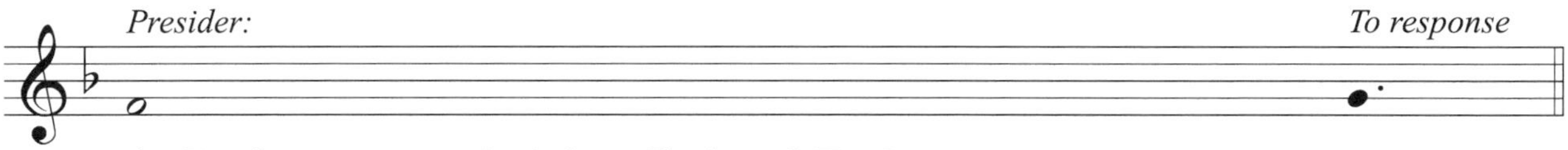


1. **Praise to you, almighty God and Father,
for you have created water to cleanse and give life.**
2. **Praise to you, Lord Jesus Christ, the Father's only Son,
for you offered yourself on the cross,**
3. **that in the blood and water flowing from your side
and through your death and resurrection
the Church might be born.**
4. **Praise to you, God the Holy Spirit,
for you anointed Christ at his baptism
in the waters of the Jordan,
that we might all be baptized in you.**
5. **Come to us, Lord, Father of all,
and make holy this water which you have cre - ated,**
6. **so that all who are baptized in it
may be washed clean of sin
and be born again to live as your children.**
7. **Make this water holy, Lord,
so that all who are baptized
into Christ's death and resurrection by this water
may become more perfectly like your Son.**

*If there is water to be blessed, the presider touches the water with his right hand and continues with verse 8:*
*OR*
*During the Easter season, if the water has already been blessed, verse 8 is omitted and the presider concludes with the spoken* Concluding Prayer *on the next page*:

**Response**

**Verse 8**

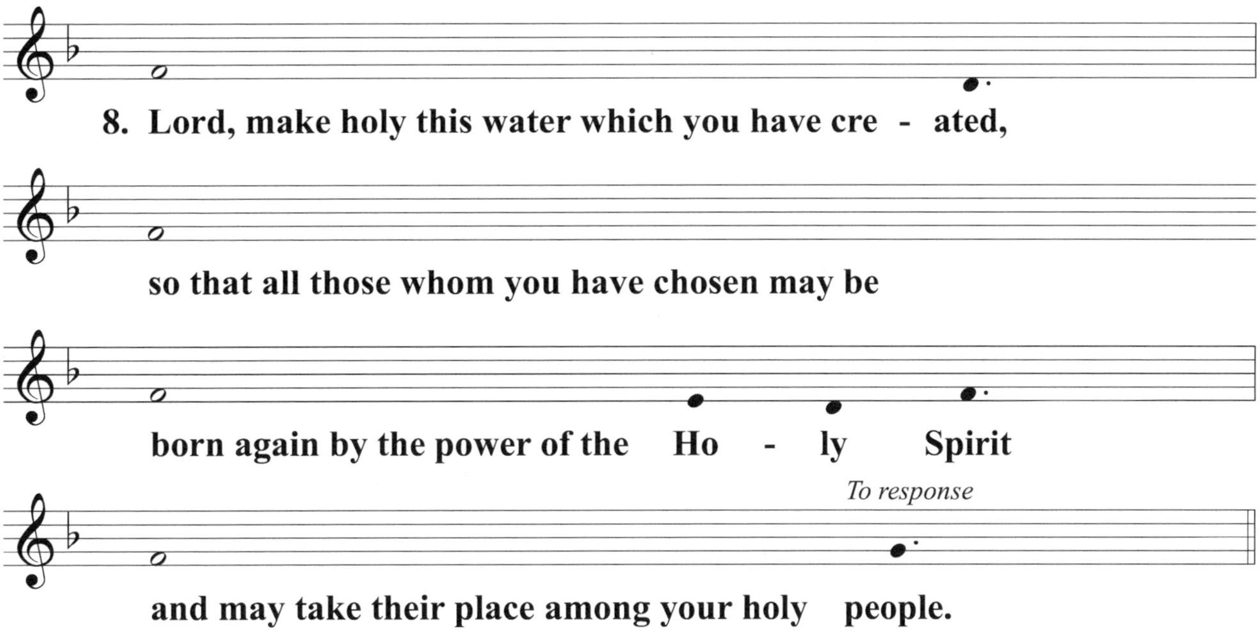


**Response**

**Concluding Prayer**

**Presider:** **You have called your children, *N.* and *N.*, to this cleansing water,**
**that they may share in the faith of your Church and have eternal life.**
**By the mystery of this consecrated water**
**lead them to a new and spiritual birth.**
**We ask this through Christ our Lord.**

**All:** Amen.

**Performance Notes**
*This litany form could be adapted for use with many other texts.*

## Reprint Policy

Before reproducing the assembly graphics on pages 56–64, you must secure the appropriate Reprint License. By using this copyrighted material, you have a moral obligation to the composers whose livelihood depends on receiving a fair compensation for the use of their work. We trust that you value their work and will agree to this requirement. The following Reprint License options are available: 1) the purchase of a $35.00 Annual Reprint License from Liturgical Press (the reporting of titles is not required when reproduced; 2) membership with the licensing service OneLicense.net (you must report the use of titles each time they are reproduced). Each reprint must include the title and the full copyright notice as it appears below the music.

### Apostles' Creed (Latin)

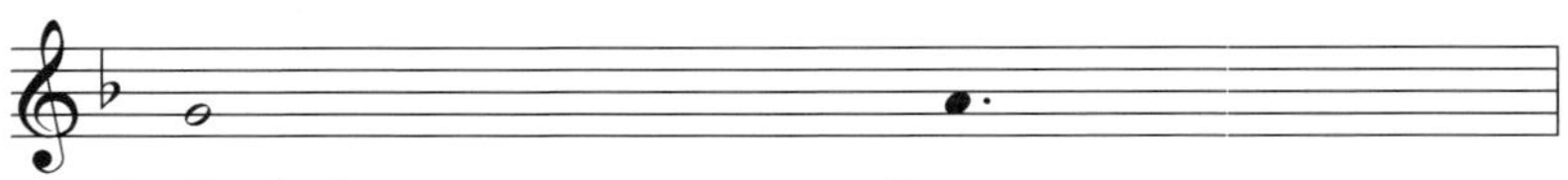

1. Credo in unum Deum,
2. et in Iesum Christum,
3. qui concéptus est de Spíritu Sancto,
4. passus sub Póntio Pi - láto,
5. descéndit ad ínferos,
6. ascéndit ad cælos,
7. inde ven - túrus est
8. Credo in Spíritum Sanctum,
9. sanctórum communi - ónem,
10. carnis resurrecti - ónem,

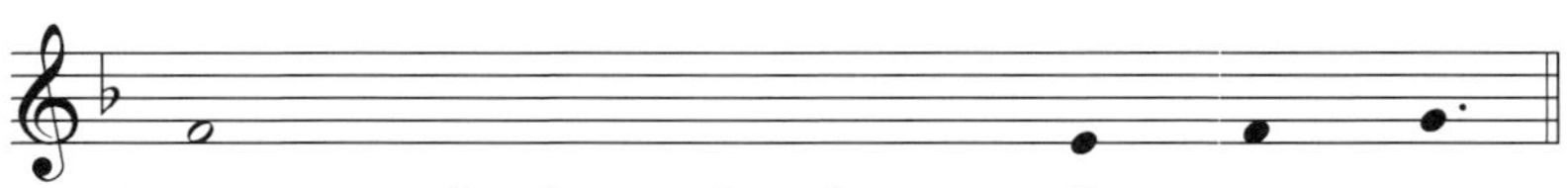

1. Patrem omnipoténtem, Creatórem cæ - li et terrae,
2. Filium eius únicum, Dó - mi - num nostrum,
3. natus ex Ma - rí - a Vírgine,
4. crucifíxus, mórtuus, et se - púltus,
5. tértia die resurréx - it a mórtuis,
6. sedet ad déxteram Dei Patris om - ni - po - téntis,
7. iudicáre vi - vos et mórtuos.
8. sanctam Ecclési - am ca - thólicam,
9. remissiónem pec - ca - tórum,
10. vitam ætér - nam. A - men.

From *You Will Be My Witnesses: Music for Christian Initiation.*
Text: *Missale Romanum.*


### Apostles' Creed (English)

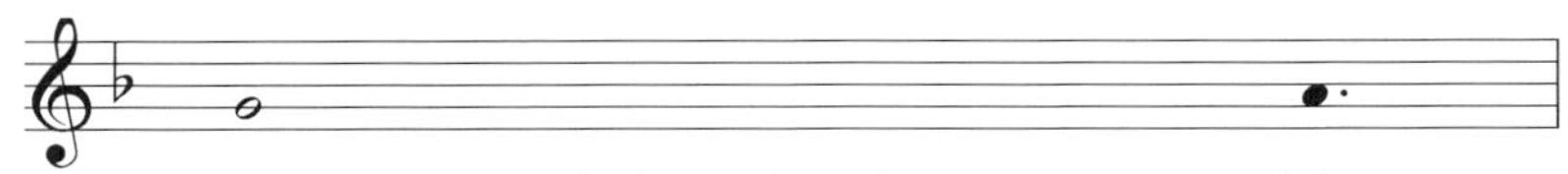

1. I believe in God, the Father al - mighty,
2. I believe in Jesus Christ, his only Son, our Lord.
3. He suffered under Pontius Pilate,
4. He descended to the dead.
5. He ascended into heaven,
6. He will come a - gain
7. I believe in the Holy Spirit,
8. the communion of saints, the forgiveness of sins,

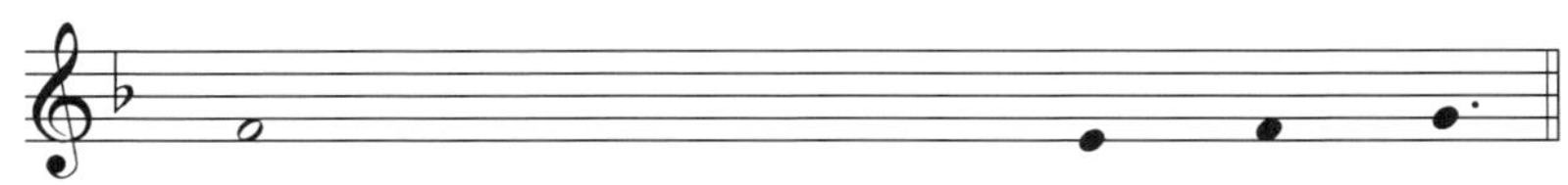

1. creator of hea - ven and earth.
2. He was conceived by the power of the Holy Spirit and born of the Vir - gin Mary.
3. was crucified, died, and was buried.
4. On the third day he rose a - gain.
5. and is seated at the right hand of the Father.
6. to judge the living and the dead.
7. the holy ca - tho - lic Church,
8. the resurrection of the body, and the life everlast - ing. A - men.

From *You Will Be My Witnesses: Music for Christian Initiation.*

See page 56 for reprint policy.

## Apostles' Creed (Spanish)

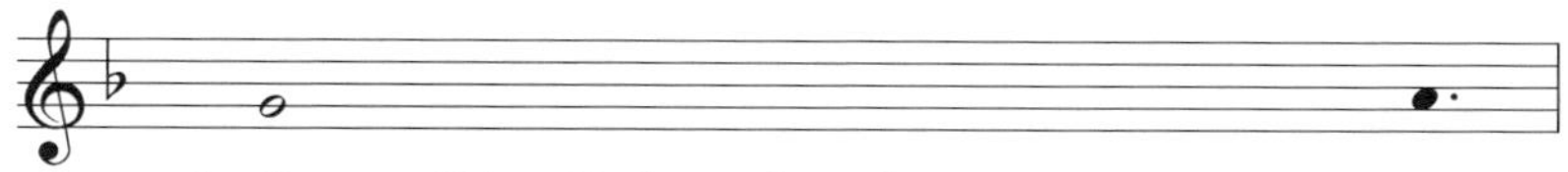

1. Creo en Dios, Padre todopode - roso,
2. Creo en Jesu - cristo,
3. que fue concebido por obra y gracia del Espíritu Santo,
4. padeció bajo el poder de Poncio Pi - lato,
5. descendió a los in - fiernos,
6. subió a los cielos
7. Desde allí ha de ve - nir
8. Creo en el Espíritu Santo,
9. la comunión de los santos,
10. la resurrección de la carne

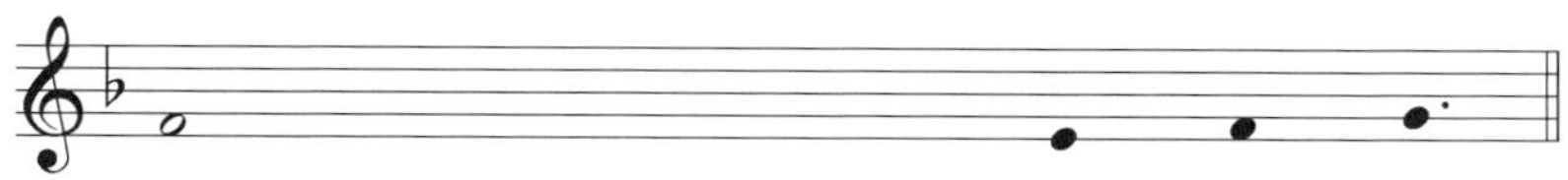

1. Creador del cielo y de la tierra.
2. su único Hijo, nue - stro Se - ñor,
3. nació de santa Ma - rí - a Virgen,
4. fue crucificado, muerto y se - pul - tado,
5. al tercer día resucitó de en - tre los muertos,
6. y está sentado a la derecha de Dios, Padre todo - po - de - roso.
7. a juzgar a vi - vos y muertos.
8. la santa Iglesi - a ca - tólica,
9. el perdón de los pe - cados,
10. y la vida eter - na. A - mén.

From *You Will Be My Witnesses: Music for Christian Initiation.*


## Come, Children, Listen to Me

From *You Will Be My Witnesses: Music for Christian Initiation,* 

## Glory to You, Lord Jesus Christ

From *You Will Be My Witnesses: Music for Christian Initiation,* 

## Go in Peace

From *You Will Be My Witnesses: Music for Christian Initiation,* 

See page 56 for reprint policy.

## Litany of the Saints

From *You Will Be My Witnesses: Music for Christian Initiation.*
Text: *Litany of the Saints,* © 1973, International Commission on English in the Liturgy, Inc., adapt.
Music: © 2010, The Collegeville Composers Group,
published and administered by Liturgical Press, Collegeville, MN 56321. 

## Litany of the Saints, Alternate Opening Dialogue

From *You Will Be My Witnesses: Music for Christian Initiation.*
Text: *Litany of the Saints,* © 1973, International Commission on English in the Liturgy, adapt.
Music: © 2010, The Collegeville Composers Group,
published and administered by Liturgical Press, Collegeville, MN 56321. 

See page 56 for reprint policy.

## Lord, Listen to Our Prayer

Response

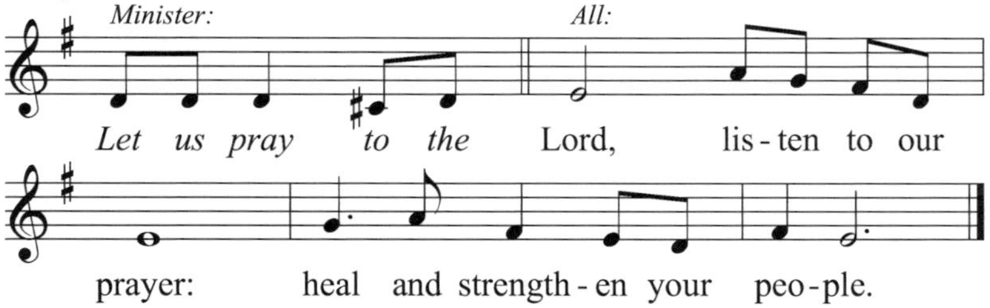


From *You Will Be My Witnesses: Music for Christian Initiation,* 

**Or**

Response

From *You Will Be My Witnesses: Music for Christian Initiation,* 

## The Lord's Prayer (Latin)

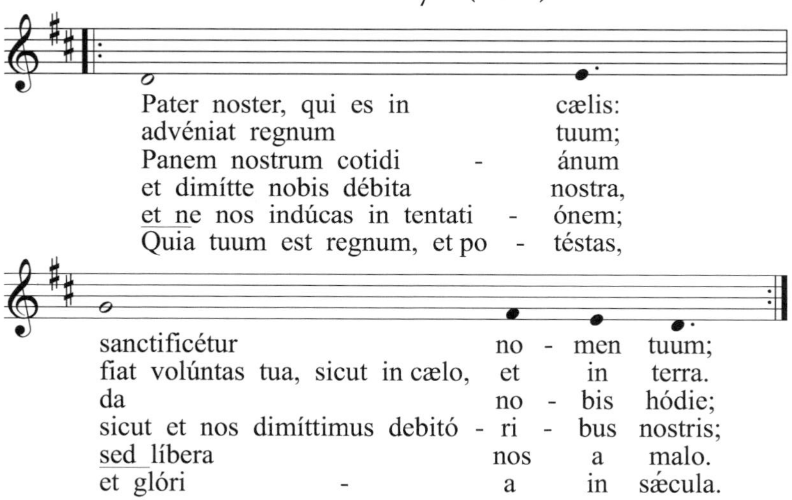


From *You Will Be My Witnesses: Music for Christian Initiation.*
Text: *Missale Romanum.* Music: 

## The Lord's Prayer (English, Traditional Embolism Acclamation)

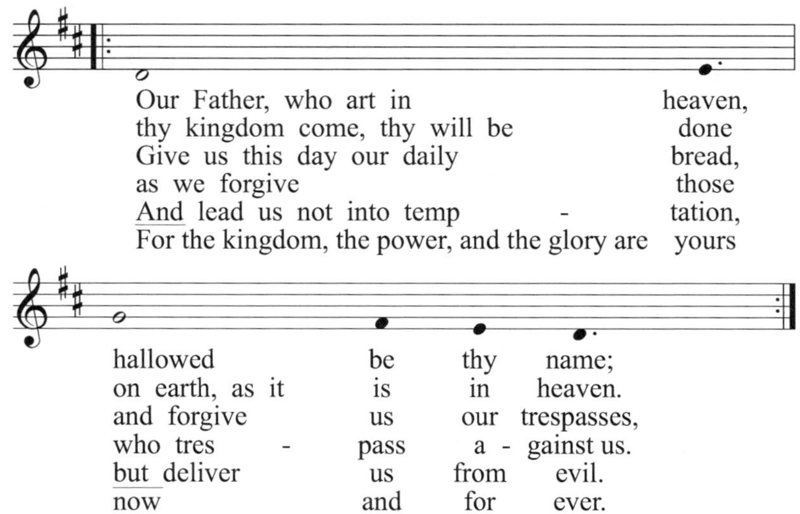


From *You Will Be My Witnesses: Music for Christian Initiation.*
Text: American edition of the *Book of Common Prayer,* 1790, adapt. from the Anglican *Book of Common Prayer,* 1549.
Music: 

## The Lord's Prayer (English, Anglican Embolism Acclamation)

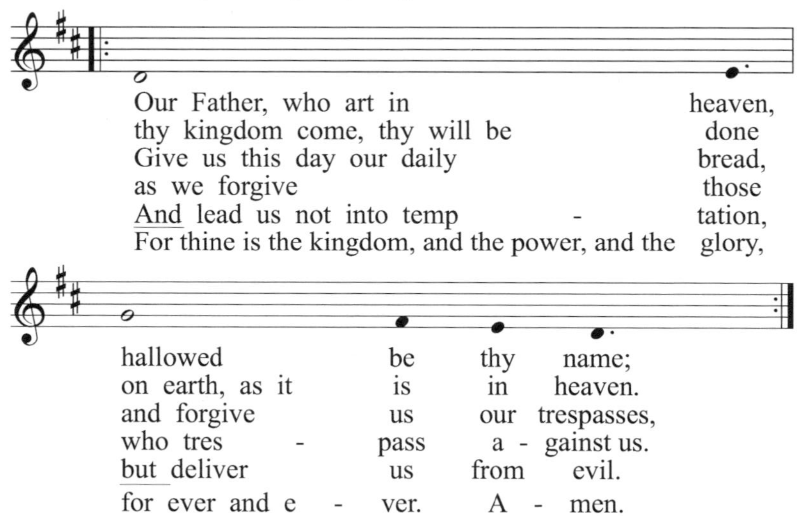


From *You Will Be My Witnesses: Music for Christian Initiation.*
Text: American edition of the *Book of Common Prayer,* 1790, adapt. from the Anglican *Book of Common Prayer,* 1549.
Embolism acclamation, © 1979, Charles Mortimer Guilbert, custodian of the standard *Book of Common Prayer.*
Music: 

**See page 56 for reprint policy.**

## The Lord's Prayer (Modern English, ecumenical)

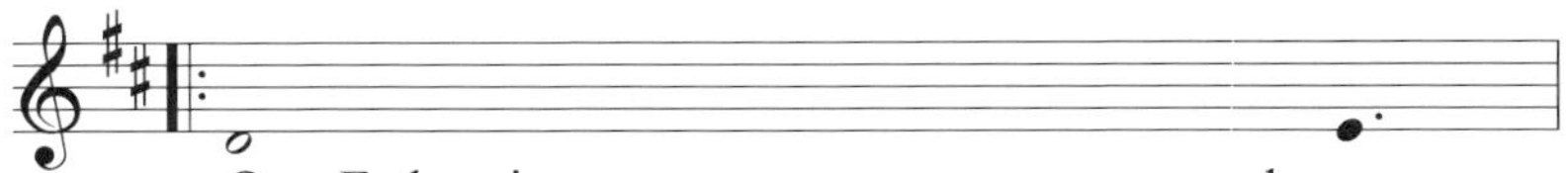

Our Father in heaven,
your kingdom come, your will be done,
Give us today our daily bread.
as we forgive those
Save us from the time of trial
For the kingdom, the power, and the glory are yours

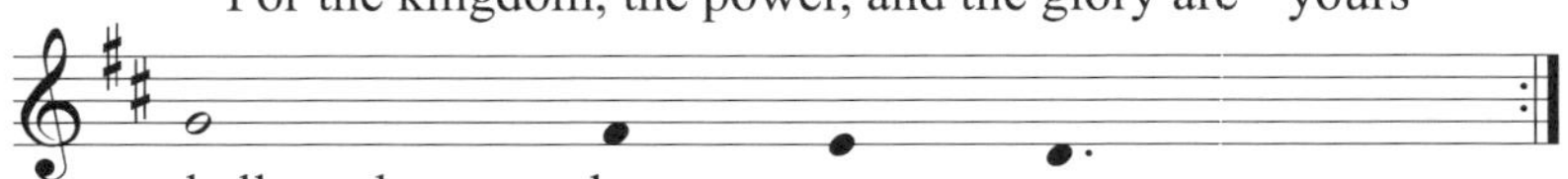

hallowed be your name,
on earth as in heaven.
Forgive us our sins
who sin a - gainst us.
and deliver us from evil.
now and for ever.

From *You Will Be My Witnesses: Music for Christian Initiation.*


## The Lord's Prayer (Spanish)

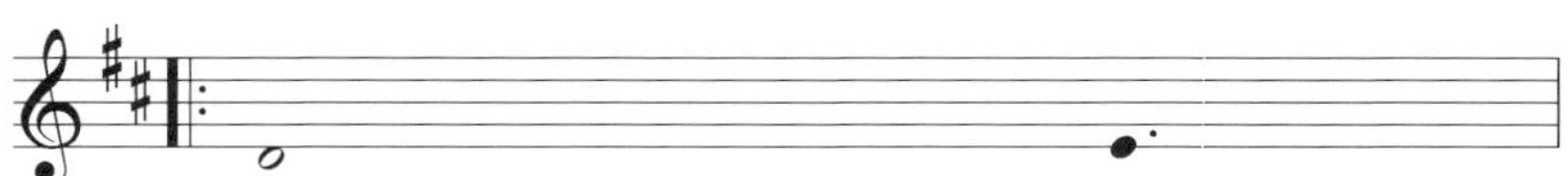

Padre nuestro, que estás en el cielo,
venga a nosotros tu reino;
Danos hoy nuestro pan de cada día;
como también nosotros perdo - namos
no nos dejes caer en la tenta - ción,
Tuyo es el reino, tuyo el poder y la gloria,

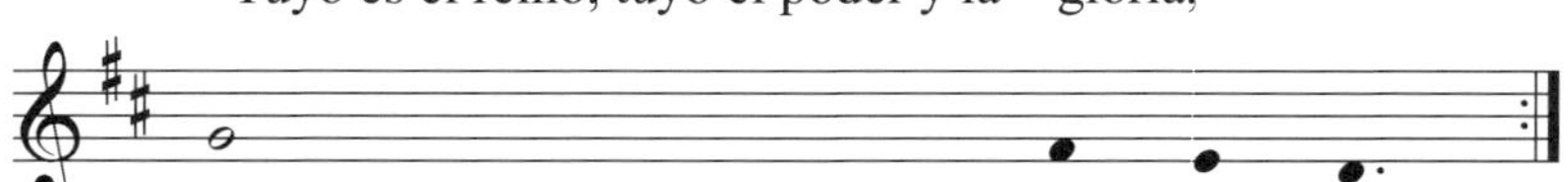

santificado sea tu Nombre;
hágase tu voluntad en la tierra como en el cielo.
perdona nue - stras o - fensas,
a los que nos o - fenden;
y líbra - nos del mal.
por siem - pre, Se - ñor.

From *You Will Be My Witnesses: Music for Christian Initiation.*


## The Lord's Prayer (French)

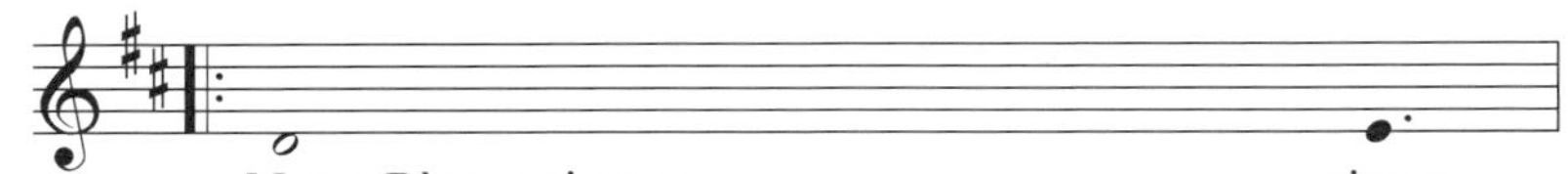

Notre Père, qui es aux cieux,
que ton règne vienne, que ta volonté soit faite
Donne-nous aujourd'hui notre pain de ce jour;
comme nous pardonnons aus - si
Et ne nous soumets pas à la tenta - tion,
Car c'est à toi qui appartiennent le règne,
la puissance et la gloire

que ton nom soit sanc - ti - fié,
sur la terre comme au ciel.
pardonne-nous nos of - fenses,
à ceux qui nous ont of - fen - sés.
mais délivre - nous du mal.
pour les siè - cles des siècles.

From *You Will Be My Witnesses: Music for Christian Initiation.*


## Lord, We Praise You

Response

Lord, we praise you; Lord, we bless you.

From *You Will Be My Witnesses: Music for Christian Initiation,* 

See page 56 for reprint policy.

## Nicene Creed (Latin)

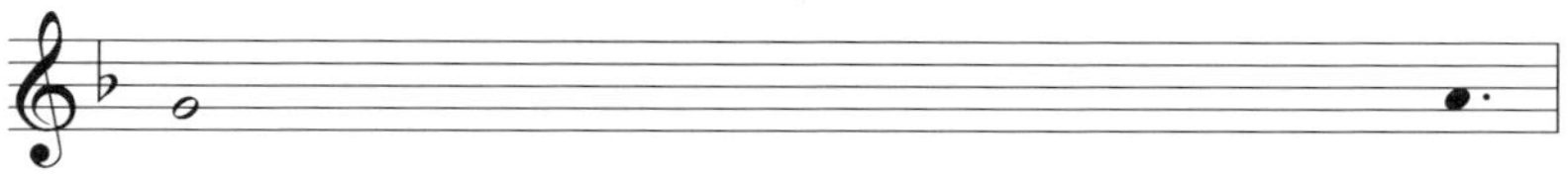

1. Credo in unum Deum,
2. factórem cæli et terrae,
3. Et in unum Dóminum Iesum Christum, Fílium Dei Uni-génitum,
4. Deum de Deo, lumen de lúmine,
5. génitum, non factum,
6. Qui propter nos hómines et propter nostram sa - lútem
7. Et incarnátus est de Spíritu Sancto ex María Vírgine,
8. Crucifíxus étiam pro nobis sub Póntio Pi - láto;
9. et resurréxit tértia die,
10. et ascéndit in cælum,
11. Et íterum ventúrus est cum glória, iudicáre vivos et mórtuos,
12. Et in Spíritum Sanctum, Dóminum et vivifi - cántem:
13. Qui cum Patre et Fílio simul adorátur et conglorifi - cátur:
14. Et unam, sanctam, ca - thólicam
15. Confíteor unum bap - tísma
16. Et exspécto resurréctionem mortu - órum,

1. Patrem om - ni - po - téntem,
2. visibílium omnium et in - vi - si - bílium.
3. et ex Patre natum ante óm - ni - a sæcula.
4. Deum verum de De - o vero,
5. consubstantiálem Patri: per quem ómnia fa - cta sunt.
6. descén - dit de cælis.
7. et homo fa - ctus est.
8. passus et se - púltus est.
9. secún - dum Scrip - túras,
10. sedet ad déx - te - ram Patris.
11. cuius regni non e - rit finis.
12. qui ex Patre Filió - que pro - cédit.
13. qui locútus est per pro - phétas.
14. et apostóli - cam Ec - clésiam.
15. in remissiónem pec - ca - tórum.
16. et vitam ventúri sæcu - li. A - men.

From *You Will Be My Witnesses: Music for Christian Initiation.*
Text: *Missale Romanum.* Music: © 2010, The Collegeville Composers Group,
published and administered by Liturgical Press, Collegeville, MN 56321. 

## Nicene Creed (English)

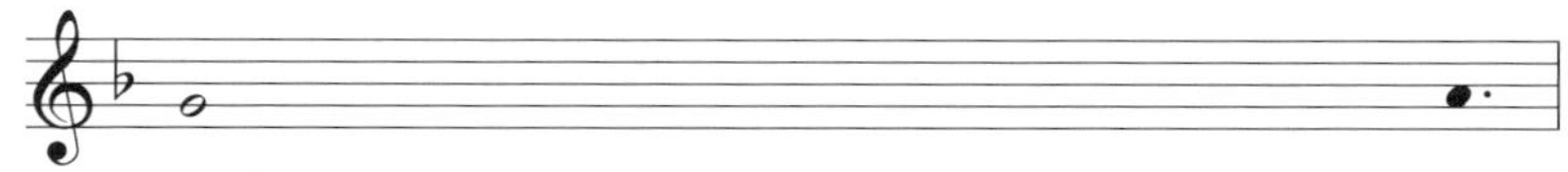

1. We believe in one God,
2. maker of heaven and earth,
3. We believe in one Lord, Jesus Christ, the only Son of God,
4. God from God, Light from Light,
5. begotten, not made, one in Being with the Father.
6. For us men and for our sal - vation
7. by the power of the Holy Spirit he was born of the Virgin Mary,
8. For our sake he was crucified under Pontius Pilate;
9. On the third day he rose a - gain
10. he ascended into heaven
11. He will come again in glory to judge the living and the dead,
12. We believe in the Holy Spirit, the Lord, the giver of life,
13. With the Father and the Son he is worshiped and glorified.
14. We believe in one holy catholic
15. We acknowledge one baptism
16. We look for the resurrection of the dead,

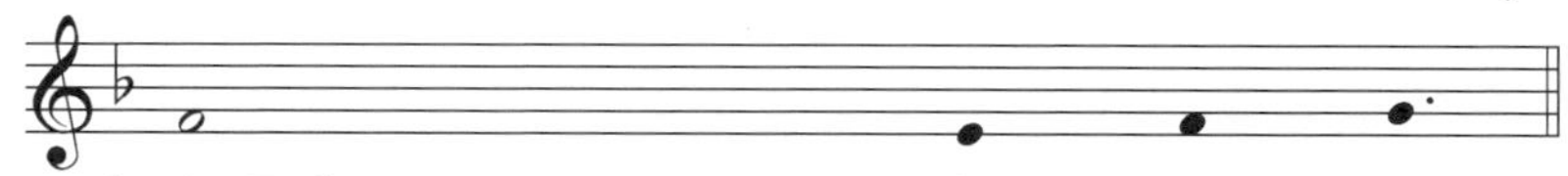

1. the Father, the Al - mighty,
2. of all that is, seen and unseen.
3. eternally begotten of the Father,
4. true God from true God,
5. Through him all things were made.
6. he came down from heaven:
7. and be - came man.
8. he suffered, died, and was buried.
9. in fulfillment of the Scriptures;
10. and is seated at the right hand of the Father.
11. and his kingdom will have no end.
12. who proceeds from the Father and the Son.
13. He has spoken through the Prophets.
14. and apo - sto - lic Church.
15. for the forgive - ness of sins.
16. and the life of the world to come. A - men.

From *You Will Be My Witnesses: Music for Christian Initiation.*

See page 56 for reprint policy.

## Nicene Creed (Spanish)

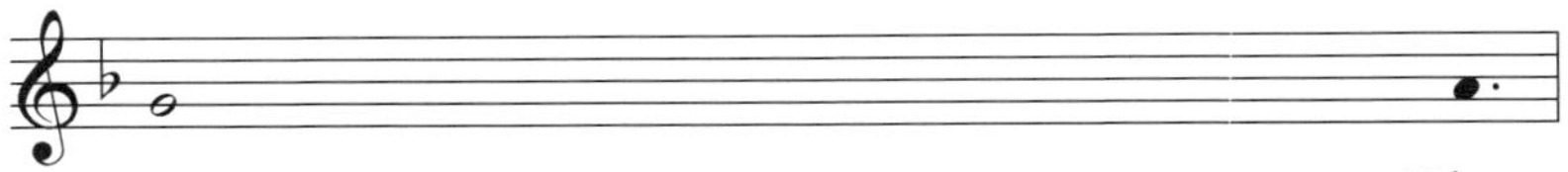

1. Creo en solo Dios,
2. Creador del cielo y de la tierra,
3. Creo en un solo Señor, Jesucristo, Hijo único de Dios,
4. Dios de Dios, Luz de Luz,
5. engendrado, no cre - ado,
6. que por nosotros, los hombres, y por nuestra salva - ción
7. y por obra del Espíritu Santo se encarnó de María, la Virgen,
8. y por nuestra causa fue crucificado en tiempos de Poncio Pi - lato;
9. y resucitó al tercer día,
10. y subió al cielo,
11. y de nuevo vendrá con gloria para juzgar a vivos y muertos,
12. Creo en el Espíritu Santo, Señor y dador de vida,
13. que con el Padre y el Hijo recibe una misma adoración y gloria,
14. Creo en la Ig - lesia,
15. Confieso que hay un solo bau - tismo
16. Espero la resurrección de los muertos

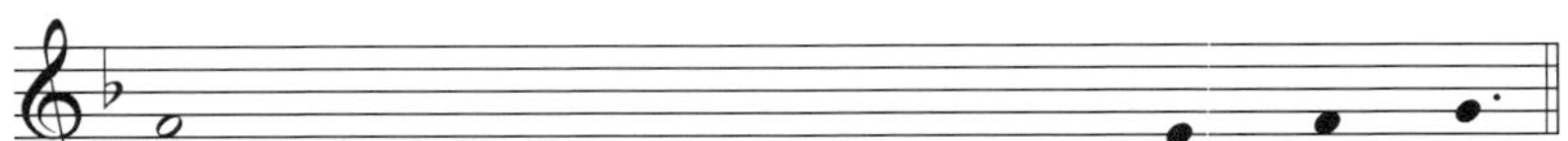

1. Padre todo - po - de - roso,
2. de todo lo visible y lo in - vi - sible.
3. nacido del Padre antes de to - los los siglos:
4. Dios verdadero de Dios ver - da - dero,
5. de la misma naturaleza del Padre, por quien to-do fue hecho;
6. ba - jó del cielo,
7. y se hi - zo hombre;
8. padeció y fue se - pul - tado,
9. según las E - scri - turas,
10. y está sentado a la dere - cha del Padre;
11. y su reino no ten - drá fin.
12. que procede del Padre y del Hijo,
13. y que habló por los pro - fetas.
14. que es una, santa, católica y a - po - stólica.
15. para el perdón de los pe - cados.
16. y la vida del mundo futu - ro. A - mén.

From *You Will Be My Witnesses: Music for Christian Initiation.*


## One Lord, One Hope, One Faith We Proclaim

From *You Will Be My Witnesses: Music for Christian Initiation,* 

## Praise to You, Alleluia

From *You Will Be My Witnesses: Music for Christian Initiation,* 

See page 56 for reprint policy.

## Taste the Goodness of the Word of God

Antiphon

## We Adore You, O Christ, and We Praise You

Refrain

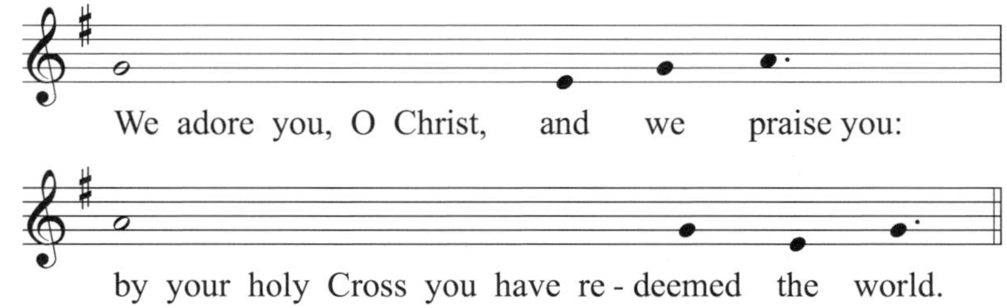


*If the concluding blessing is sung:*

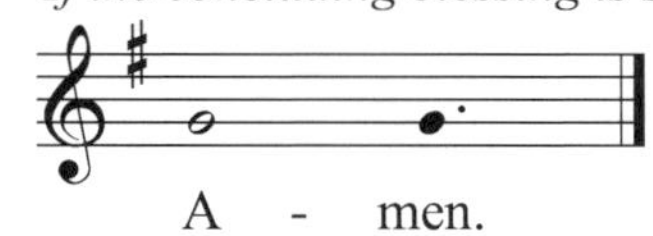




## We Adore You, O Christ, and We Bless You (for use during the Stations of the Cross)

Refrain

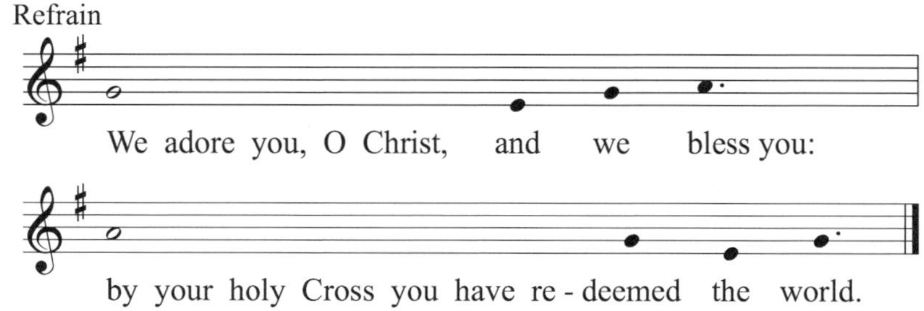

**See page 56 for reprint policy.**

## You Will Be My Witnesses